Leveled S Builders

Differentiated Practice Pages Covering Skills in These Key Areas

Language Arts

- Concepts of Print
- Phonemic Awareness
- Phonics
- Word Recognition
- Comprehension

Math

- Numbers and Operations
- Measurement
- Geometry
- Graphing
- Sorting and Patterning

Provide practice for students working at different levels!

Managing Editor: Cindy K. Daoust

Editorial Team: Becky S. Andrews, Kimberley Bruck, Karen P. Shelton, Diane Badden, Thad H. McLaurin, Sharon Murphy, Lynn Drolet, Karen A. Brudnak, Hope Rodgers, Dorothy C. McKinney

Production Team: Lisa K. Pitts, Pam Crane, Rebecca Saunders, Jennifer Tipton Cappoen, Chris Curry, Sarah Foreman, Theresa Lewis Goode, Clint Moore, Greg D. Rieves, Barry Slate, Donna K. Teal, Zane Williard, Tazmen Carlisle, Cat Collins, Marsha Heim, Amy Kirtley-Hill, Lynette Dickerson, Mark Rainey

www.themailbox.com

Manufactured in the United States
10 9 8 7 6 5 4 3 2 1

Table of Contents

Language Arts

Concepts of Print

Phonemic Awareness

Phonics

Word Recognition

Comprehension

Math

Number and Operations

Measurement

Geometry

Graphing

Sorting and Patterning

Student Performance Cards and Award

What's Inside?

This jam-packed resource contains over 70 pairs of skill-specific language arts and math practice pages. Each pair consists of one practice page that is on grade level and one practice page that is on a lower level, each with the same title and identical or very similar art. To help you easily identify the page you need, the page number for the lower-level reproducible is shown in a black circle.

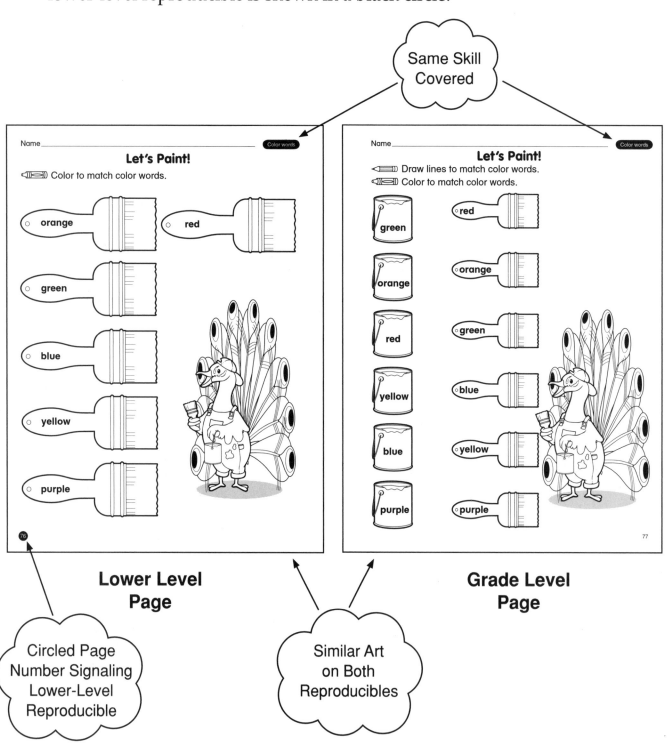

Same Skill Covered

Lower Level Page

Grade Level Page

Circled Page Number Signaling Lower-Level Reproducible

Similar Art on Both Reproducibles

How to Use

Provide differentiated skills practice for your students.

1. Scan the table of contents on pages 2 and 3 to find the skill you need.

2. Determine which practice page best suits your needs, or use both!

Use *Leveled Skill Builders* practice pages for the following:

- small-group practice
- independent practice
- whole-group practice
- remediation
- enrichment
- differentiated homework
- centers
- tutoring

Name _____

Garden of Letters

 Cut out the bees.

Match the letters.

 Glue.

Garden of Letters

 Cut out the bees.

Match the letters.

 Glue.

©The Mailbox® • *Leveled Skill Builders* • TEC61036

7

Name _____

Cheer for the Champions!

Draw a line to match partner letters.

Cheer for the Champions!

Draw a line to match partner letters.

A

I

B

Z

K

F

M

S

a

b

i

k

z

f

s

m

Name _____

10

Toys for Girls and Boys!

✂ Cut. Match the partner letters. ⬜ Glue.

J	j

F	f

B	b

M	m

K	k

D	d

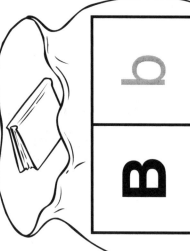
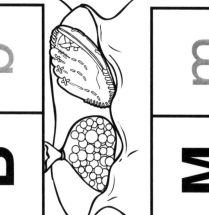

m	d	b	f	j	k

Uppercase and lowercase letters

Toys for Girls and Boys!

✂ Cut. Match the partner letters. 🍼 Glue.

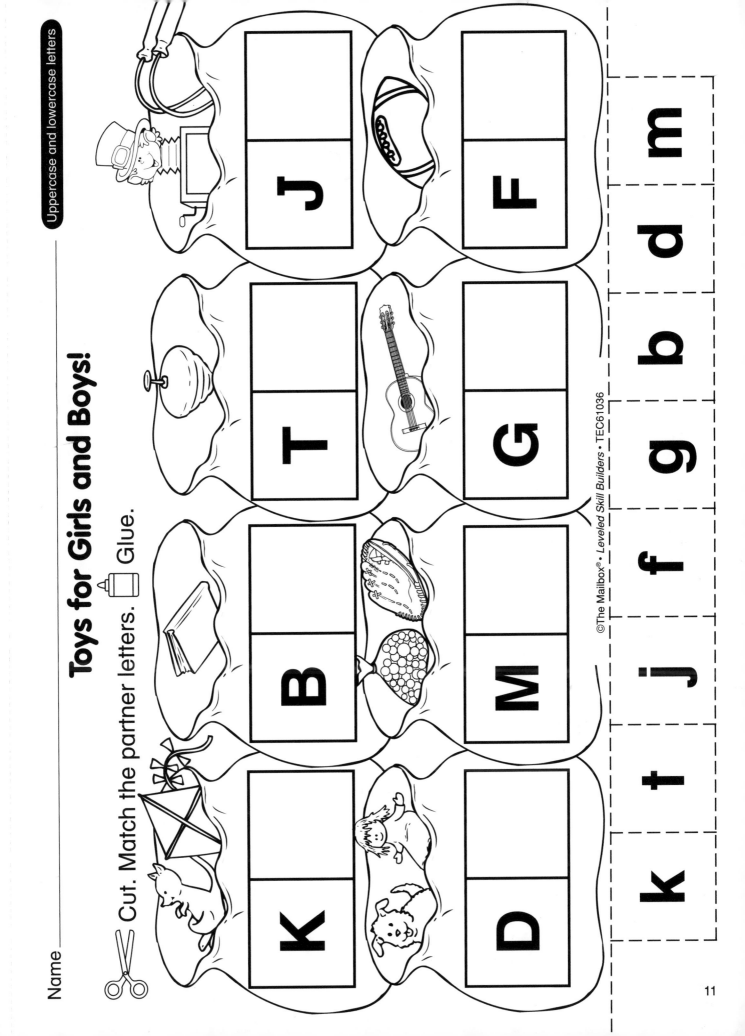

J

F

T

G

B

M

K

D

m

d

b

g

j

t

k

©The Mailbox® • Leveled Skill Builders • TEC61036

11

Toasty Toes

Trace the matching uppercase letter. Color.

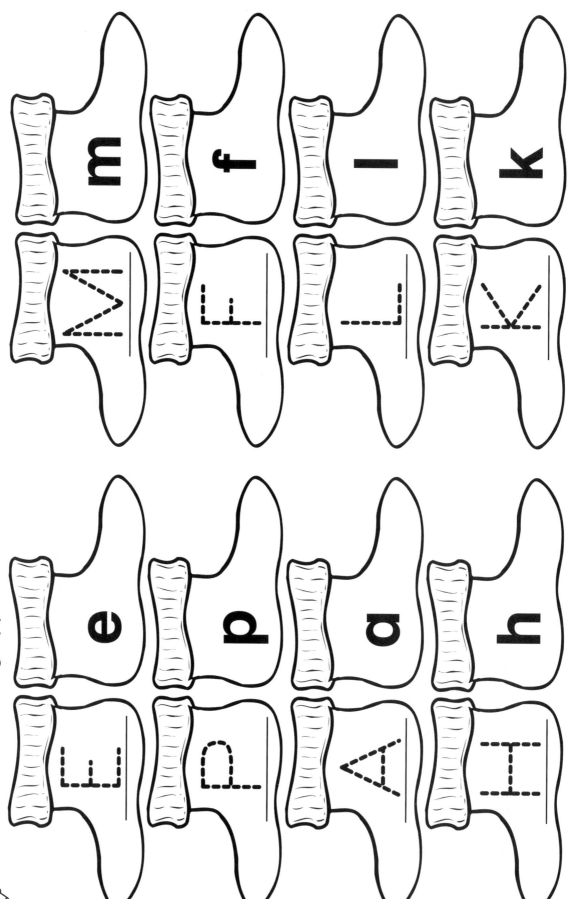

Name

Toasty Toes

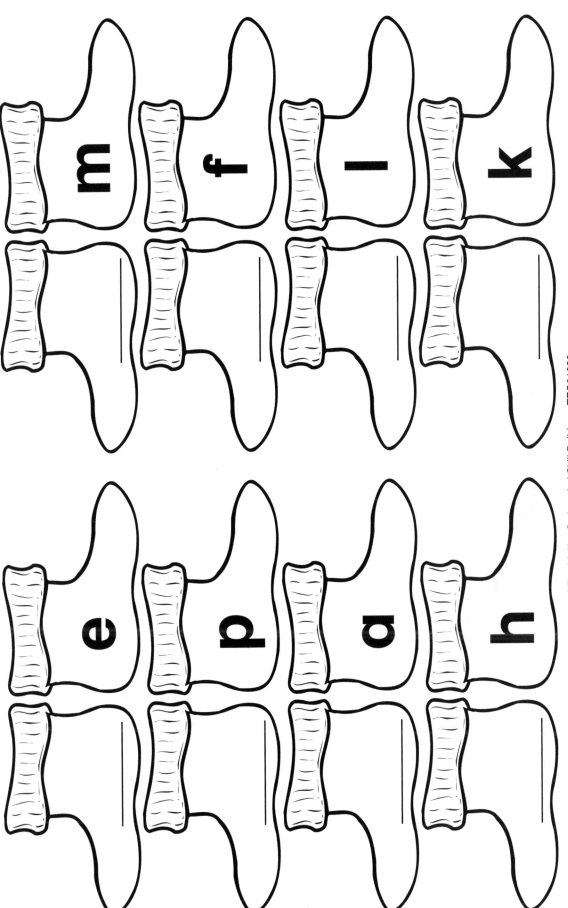

✏ Write the matching uppercase letter. 🖍 Color.

m

f

l

k

e

p

a

h

Lunchbox Rhymes

Color the lunchboxes with rhyming pictures.

Name

Lunchbox Rhymes

Color the lunchboxes with rhyming pictures.

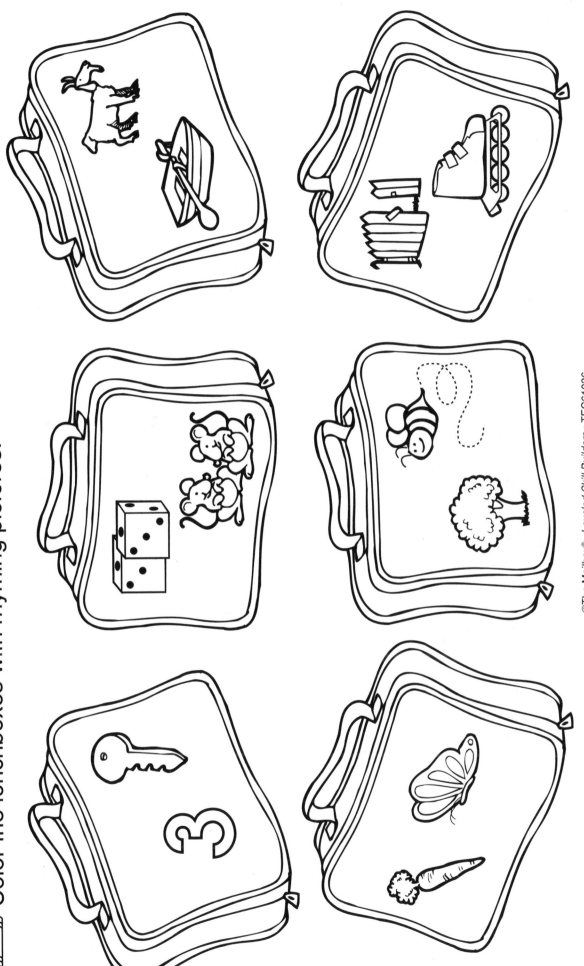

Lunch Lines

 Color the picture that rhymes.

 Draw an X on the picture that does not rhyme.

Lunch Lines

 Color the pictures that rhyme.

Draw an X on the picture that does not rhyme.

Balancing Bear

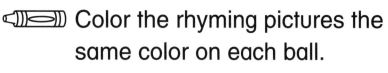 Color the rhyming pictures the same color on each ball.

Balancing Bear

Color the rhyming pictures the same color on each ball.

Performing for Peanuts

 Cut. Match the rhyming pictures.

Glue.

Performing for Peanuts

 Cut. Match the rhyming pictures.

Glue.

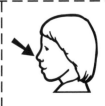

21

Maxi's Taxis

✂ Cut.

Match rhyming pictures.

Glue.

TAXI

A B

Maxi's Taxis

 Cut.

Match rhyming pictures.

 Glue.

 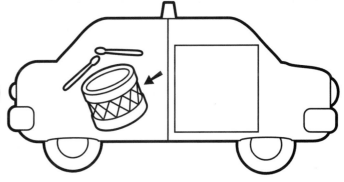

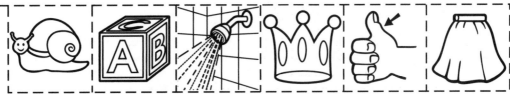

23

Name _____

Take a Cake Break

Color the rhyming pictures.

Name _____

Take a Cake Break

🖍 Color the rhyming pictures.

Name _____

Pumpkin Convoy

 Cut. Match beginning sounds. Glue.

©The Mailbox® • *Leveled Skill Builders* • TEC61036

26

Pumpkin Convoy

 Cut. Match beginning sounds. Glue.

27

Perfect Pie

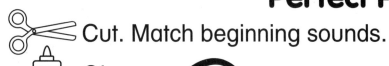

✂ Cut. Match beginning sounds.

Glue.

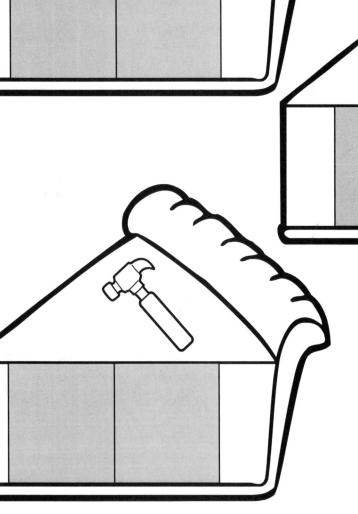

28

Perfect Pie

Cut. Match beginning sounds.

Glue.

Name _____

Tummy Yummies

 Cut. Match beginning sounds.

Glue.

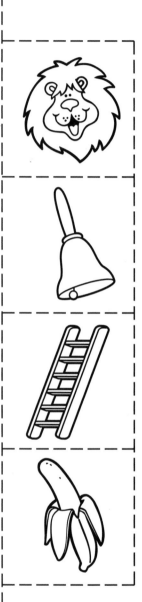

Tummy Yummies

 Cut. Match beginning sounds.

Glue.

Cookie Cook

 Cut. Match the beginning sounds.

Glue.

Name _____

Cookie Cook

 Cut. Match the beginning sounds.

Glue.

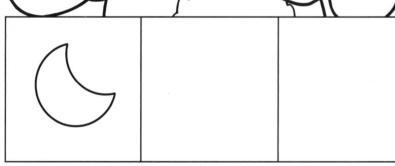

(34)

Red Light, Green Light!

✂️ Cut. Match beginning sounds. 🔺🧴 Glue.

r

g

m

p

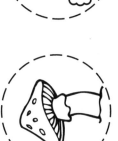
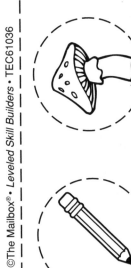

Red Light, Green Light!

✂ Cut. Match beginning sounds. 🗒 Glue.

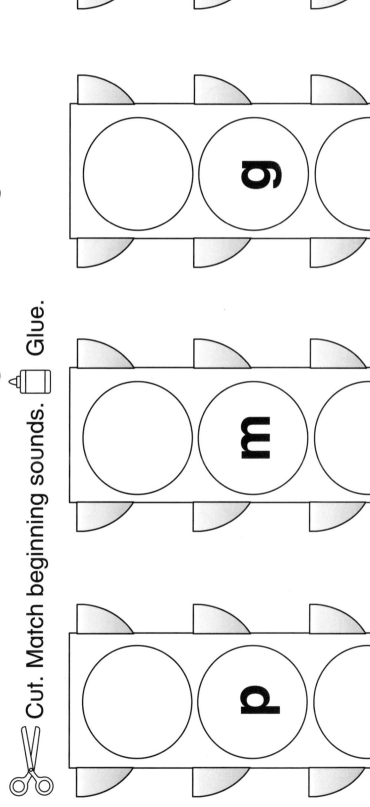

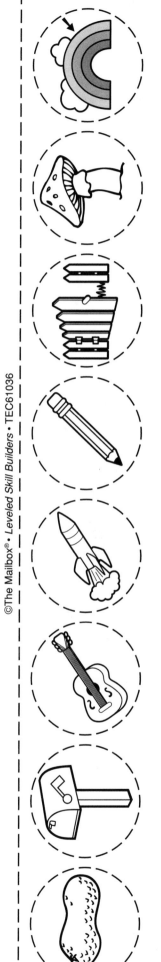

"Bear-ly" a Breeze

Color the picture with the same beginning sound.

Name_____

"Bear-ly" a Breeze

Color the pictures with the same beginning sound.

Ready, Set, Launch!

Color the pictures with the same beginning sound.

s

d

p

Name _____

Ready, Set, Launch!

Color the pictures with the same beginning sound.

s

m

d

p

Name _____

Windy Whiskers

Color the picture with the same beginning sound.

Windy Whiskers

Color the pictures with the same beginning sound.

Name

Ready for the Sun

Trace the beginning sound. Read.

pull

sand

girl

sun

kite

fish

hat

cup

ball

42

Name _____

Ready for the Sun

✏️ Write the beginning sound. Trace. Read.

43

Name _____

Leaves Galore!

 Cut.

Match beginning sounds. Glue.

44

Name

Leaves Galore!

 Cut.

Match beginning sounds. Glue.

Sky-High Fliers

Color the pictures with the same beginning sound.

Sky-High Fliers

Color the pictures with the same beginning sound.

Name _____

Cruising the Clouds

Color the pictures with the same beginning sound.

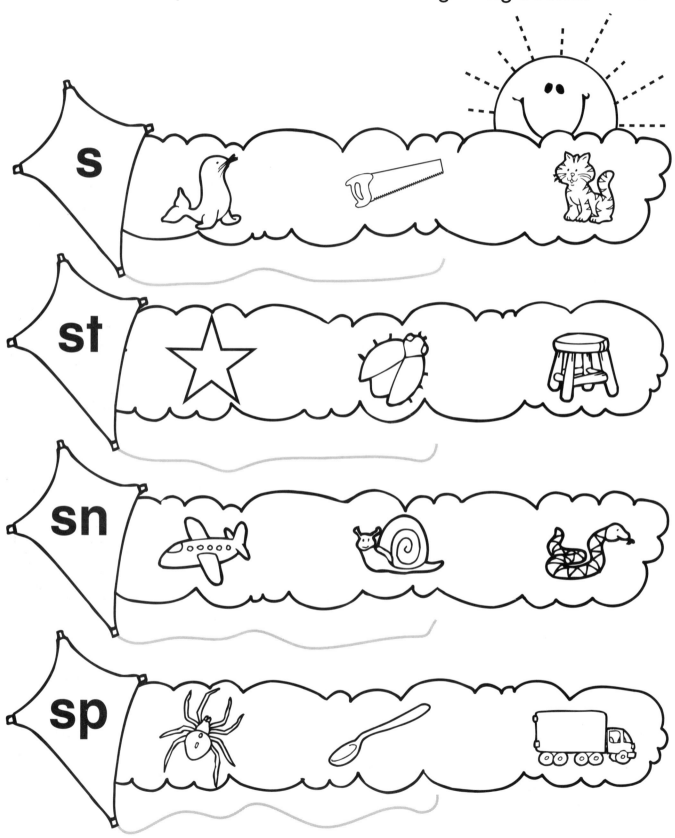

©The Mailbox® • *Leveled Skill Builders* • TEC61036

Cruising the Clouds

Color the pictures with the same beginning sound.

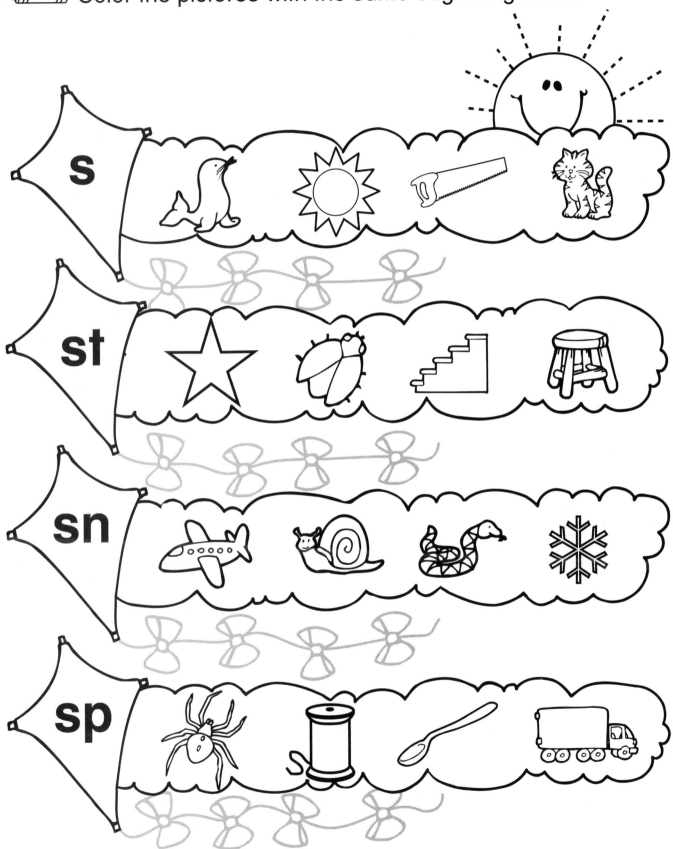

Name _____

Pots 'n' Plants

 Cut.

Match the beginning sounds. Glue.

Name _____

Pots 'n' Plants

 Cut.

Match the beginning sounds. Glue.

tr   t   tr   t   tr   t

Bandage Brigade

Name each letter and its sound.

 Cut.

Glue to match the ending sound.

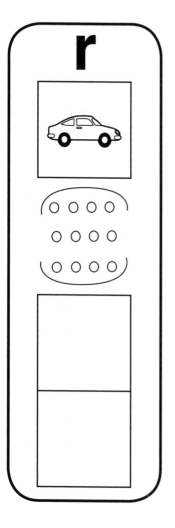

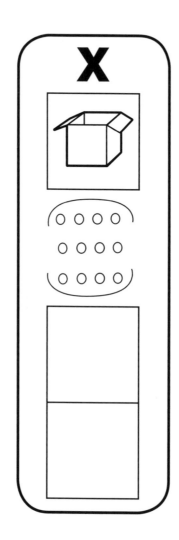

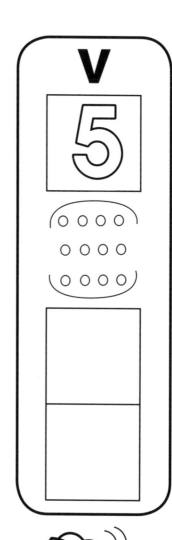

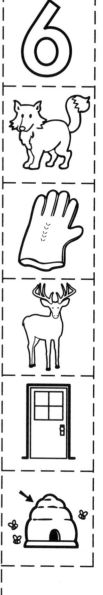

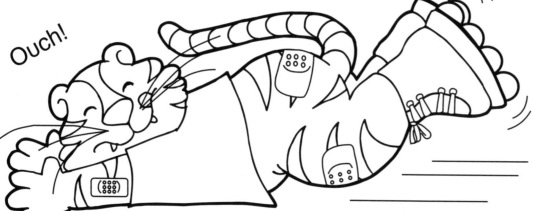

Ouch!

Bandage Brigade

Name each letter and its sound.

 Cut.

Glue to match the ending sound.

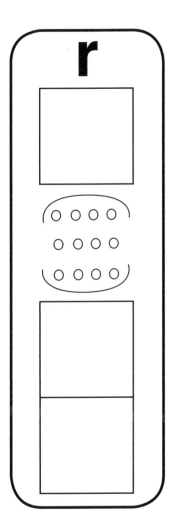

r

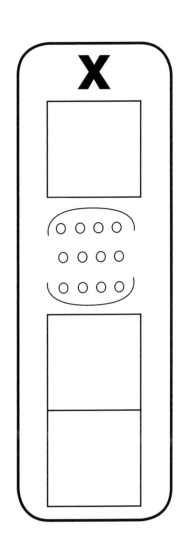

x

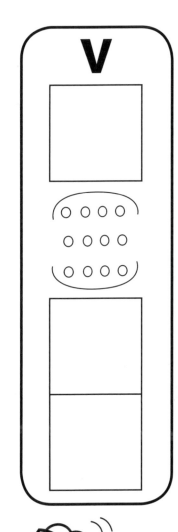

v

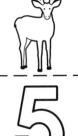

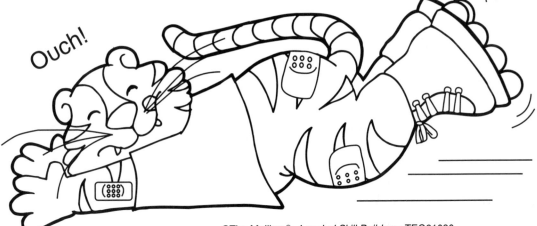

Ouch!

Name _____

Sundae Scoops

Name the picture.

Find the ending sound.

 Cut.

Glue.

f

b

s

t

m

©The Mailbox® • *Leveled Skill Builders* • TEC61036

- -

Sundae Scoops

Name the picture.

Find the ending sound.

 Cut.

Glue.

f

b

l

s

t

m

Twinkle-Toes Tiger

✏ Circle the pictures with the same ending sound.

✏ Draw an X on the picture that does not have the same ending sound.

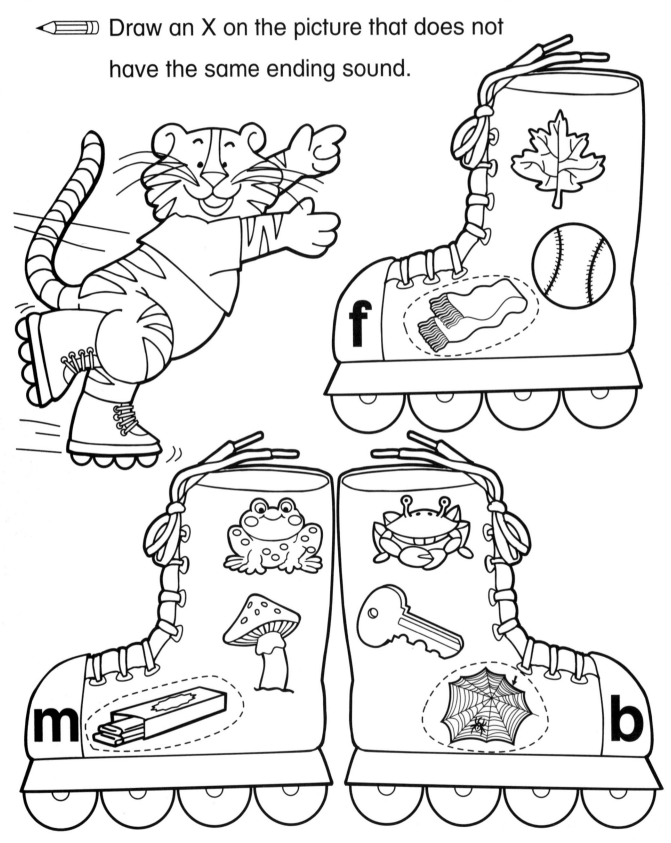

Name _____

Twinkle-Toes Tiger

Circle the pictures with the same ending sound.

Draw an X on the picture that does not

have the same ending sound.

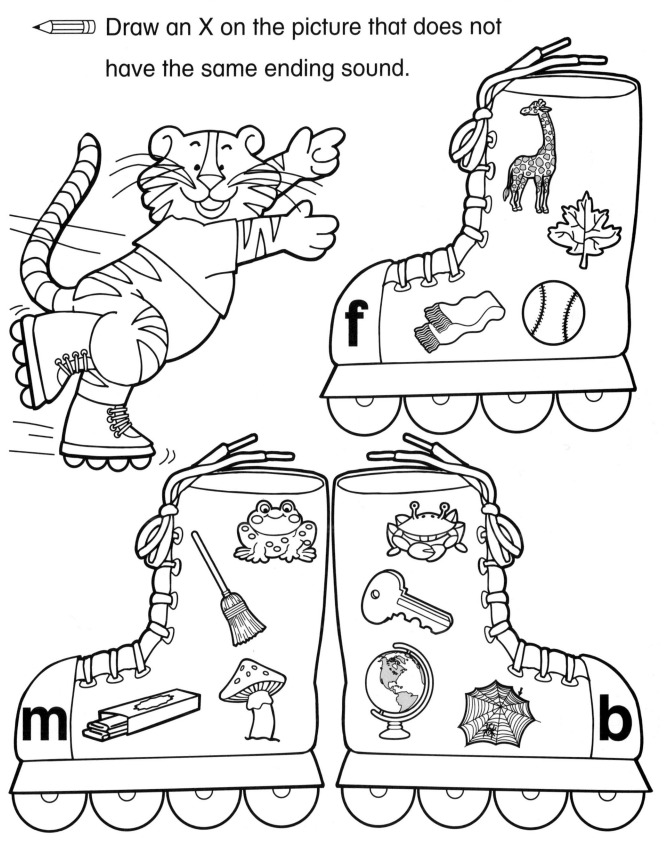

Name _____

Ticket to Roll

Name each picture.

 Trace the ending sound.

Color.

Ticket to Roll

Name each picture.

 Write the ending sound.

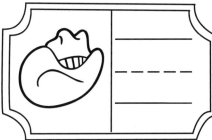 Color.

 _ _ _ _ _

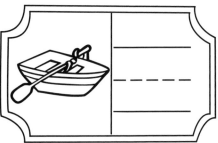 _ _ _ _ _

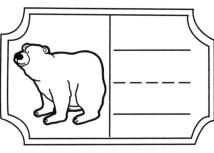 _ _ _ _ _

 _ _ _ _ _

 _ _ _ _ _

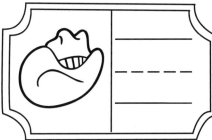 _ _ _ _ _

 _ _ _ _ _

 _ _ _ _ _

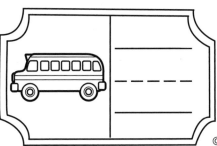 _ _ _ _ _

On a Roll!

Name each picture and say its ending sound.

 Trace the ending letter.

 Color each box as you go.

b	s	t	n	g	p	m	d	x

fo x

wi g

ha t

bi b

gu m

bu s

ca n

be d

cu p

On a Roll!

Name each picture and say its ending sound.

Write the ending letter.

Color each box as you go.

| b | s | t | n | g | p | m | d | x |

fo _ _ _ _ _

ha _ _ _ _ _

gu _ _ _ _ _

ca _ _ _ _ _

be _ _ _ _ _

cu _ _ _ _ _

wi _ _ _ _ _

bi _ _ _ _ _

bu _ _ _ _ _

Name _____

Pick a Pail

Name the picture. Find the word family.

✂ Cut.   🧴 Glue.

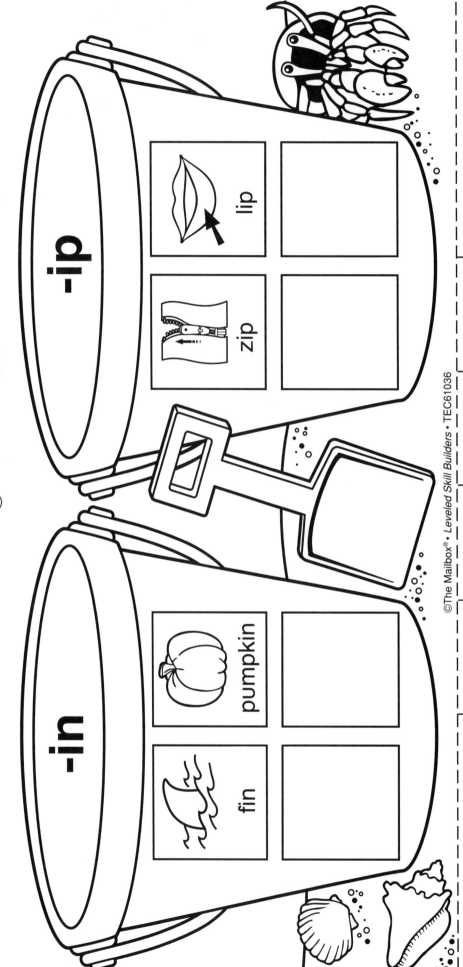

-ip

lip

zip

-in

pumpkin

fin

©The Mailbox® • *Leveled Skill Builders* • TEC61036

chin

hip

pin

ship

Word families: -in, -ip

Pick a Pail

Name the picture. Find the word family. Cut. Glue.

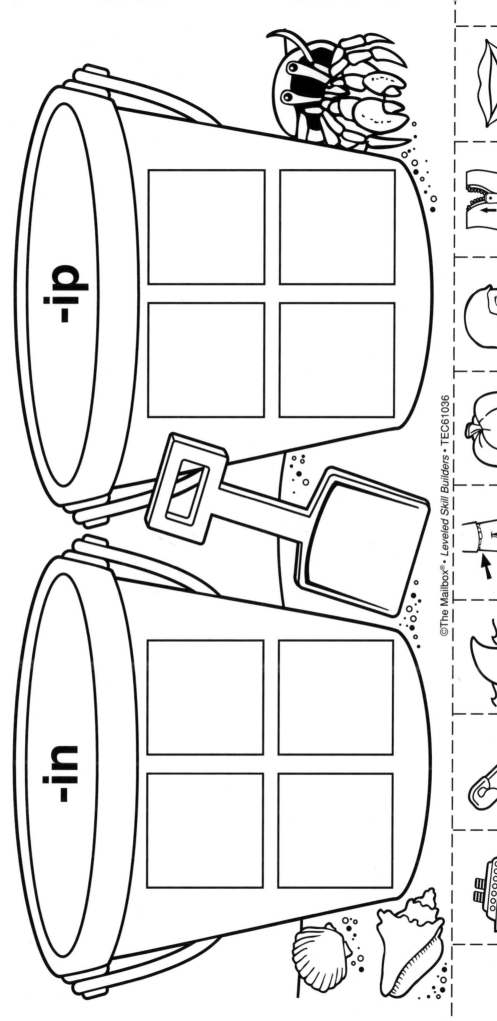

-ip

-in

©The Mailbox® • Leveled Skill Builders • TEC61036

lip

zip

chin

pumpkin

hip

fin

pin

ship

Word Launch

 Cut. Sort. Glue.

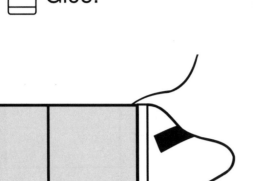

bat   cat   hat

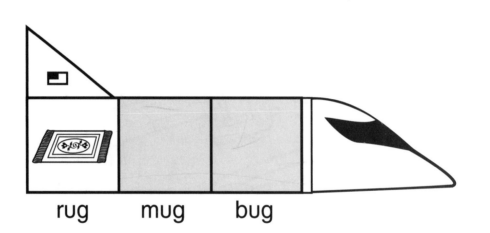

rug   mug   bug

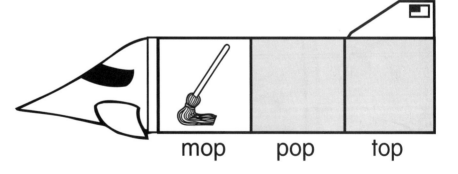

mop   pop   top

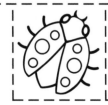     

Word Launch

✂ Cut. Sort. 🧴 Glue.

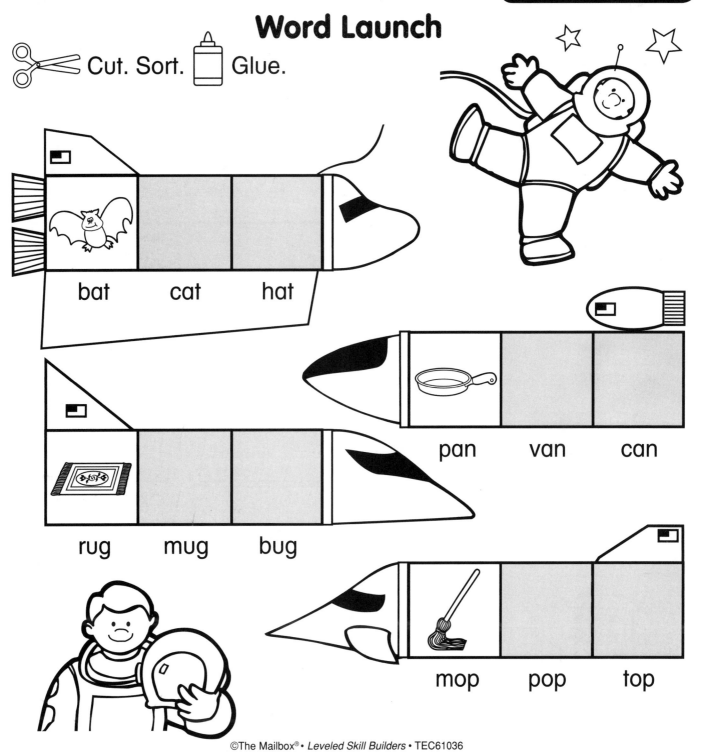

bat   cat   hat

pan   van   can

rug   mug   bug

mop   pop   top

Space Race Rhymes

✏️ Draw a line to match.

🖍️ Color.

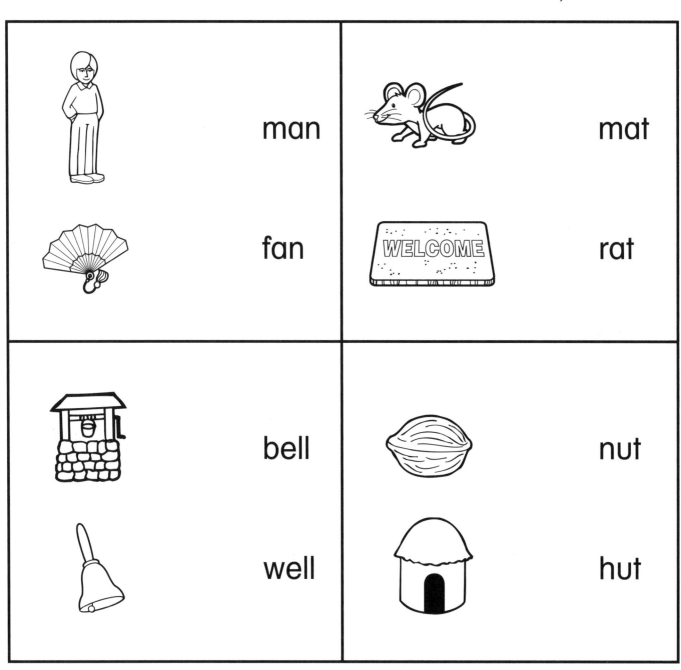

man

fan

mat

rat

bell

well

nut

hut

Space Race Rhymes

✏️ Draw a line to match.

🖍️ Color.

man

fan

mat

rat

log

dog

hop

mop

bell

well

nut

hut

Name_____

Navigate the Stars

Name each picture.

Trace.

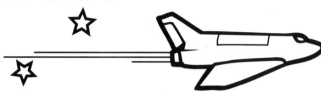

dog

log

well

bell

lip

zip

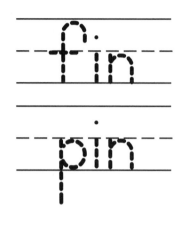

fin

pin

sun

bun

Navigate the Stars

Name each picture.

 Write the beginning letter.

Trace.

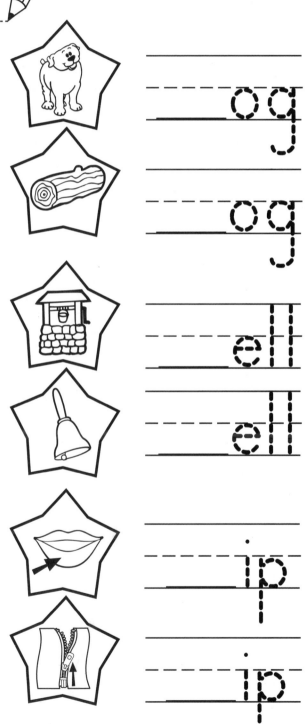

Deep Diving

Name each picture.

✏ Write the correct word family.

-og
-op

frog

hop

j ___

m ___

p ___

l ___

Name

Deep Diving

Name each picture.

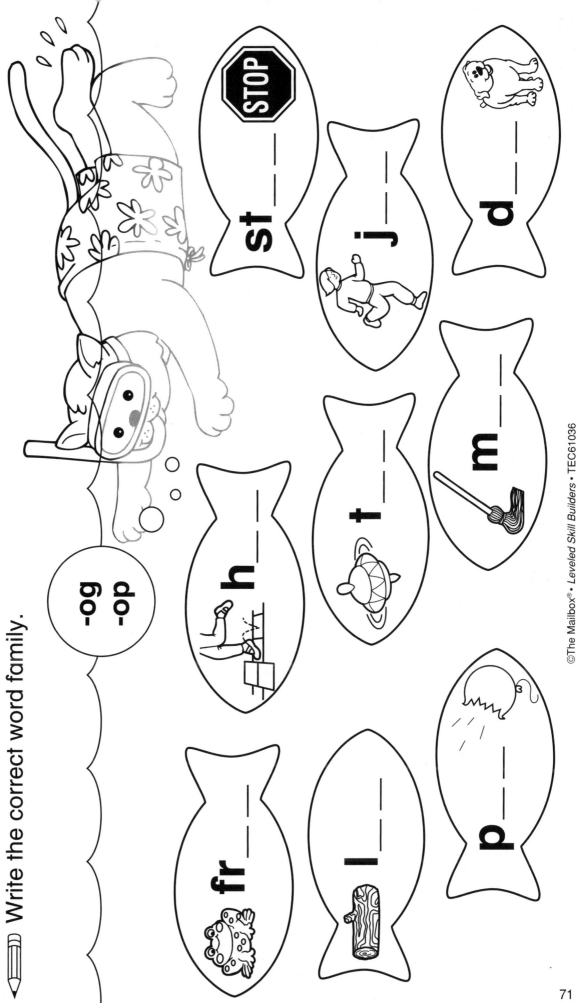

✏ Write the correct word family.

-og
-op

st ___

j ___

d ___

h ___

t ___

m ___

fr ___

l ___

p ___

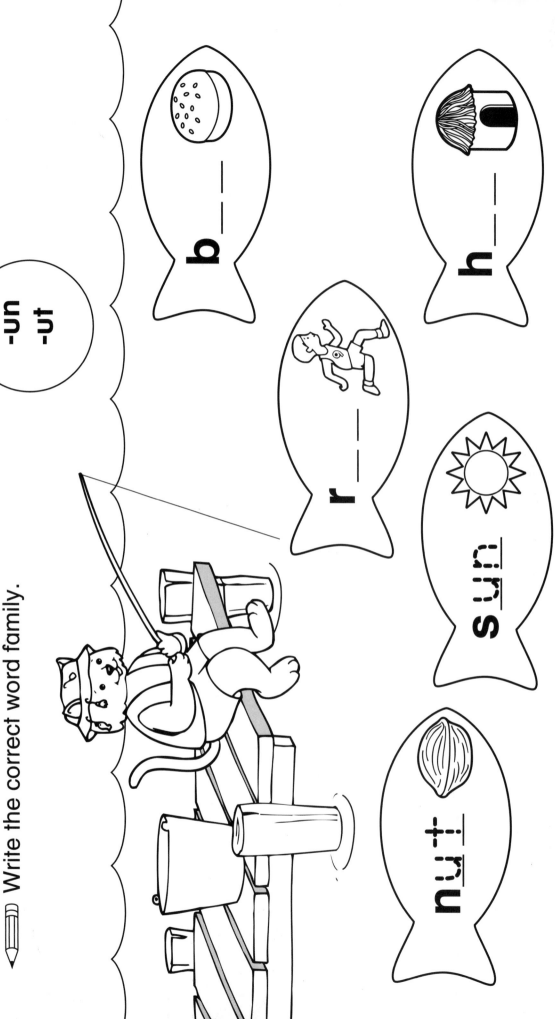

Name _____

Swim Away!

Name each picture.

✏️ Write the correct word family.

-un
-ut

b _ _

h _ _

r _ _

s u n

n u t

Swim Away!

Name each picture.

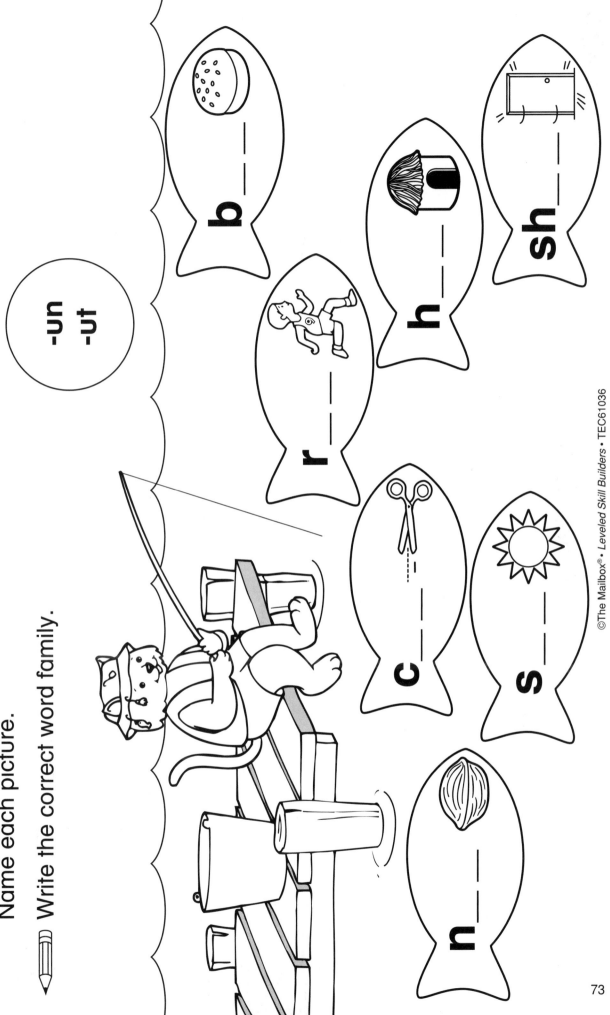

Write the correct word family.

-un
-ut

b ___ ___

h ___ ___

sh ___ ___

r ___ ___

c ___ ___

s ___ ___

n ___ ___

Scoop 'em Up!

✏️ Write.

c __ __

m __ __

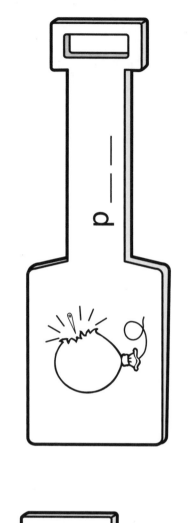

p __ __

__ l __

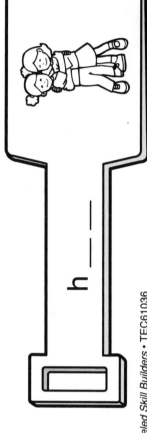

h __ __

f __ __

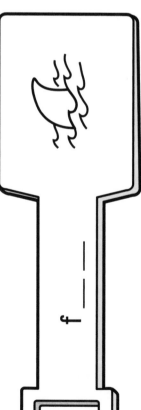

Scoop 'em Up!

✏ Write.

c

m

p

h

c

l

f

h

Let's Paint!

Color to match color words.

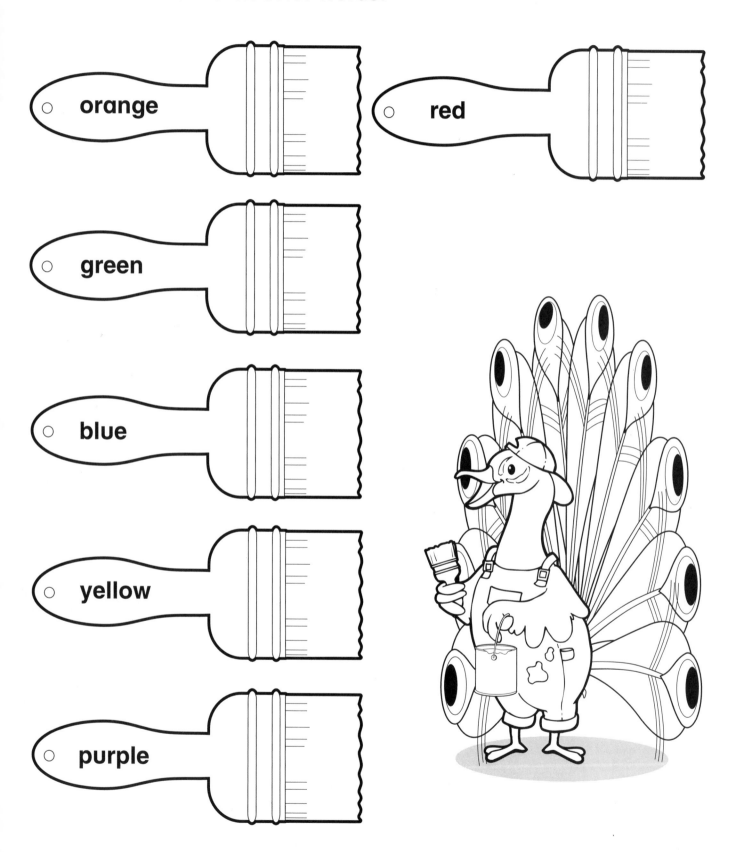

orange

red

green

blue

yellow

purple

Let's Paint!

✏️ Draw lines to match color words.
🖍️ Color to match color words.

green

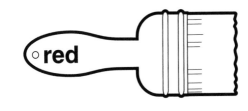
○ **red**

orange

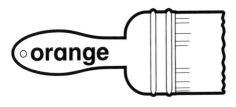
○ **orange**

red

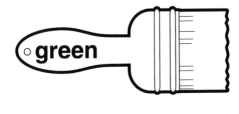
○ **green**

yellow

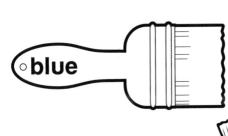
○ **blue**

blue

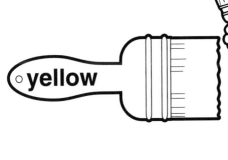
○ **yellow**

purple

○ **purple**

Mitten Match

Color to match color words.

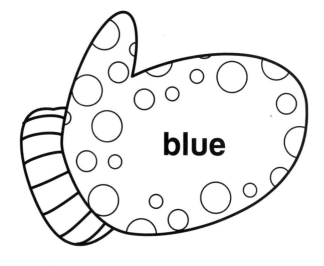

blue

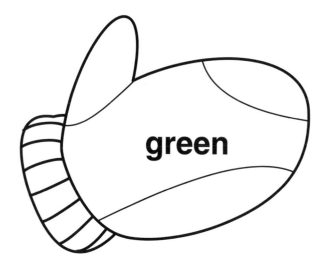

green

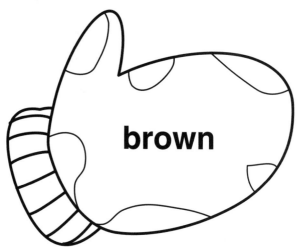

brown

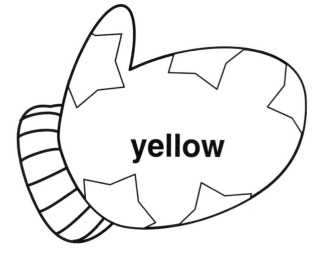

yellow

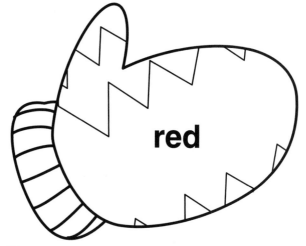

red

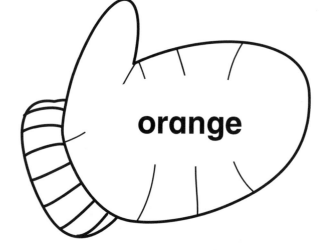

orange

Mitten Match

✏️ Draw lines to match each pair.
🖍️ Color to match color words.

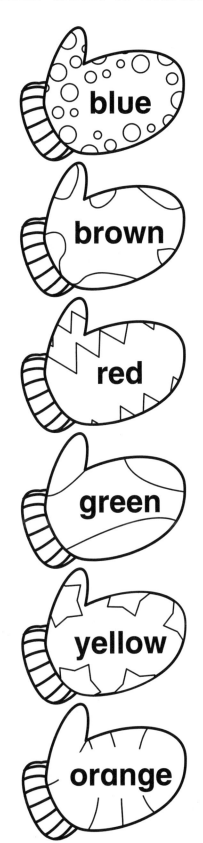
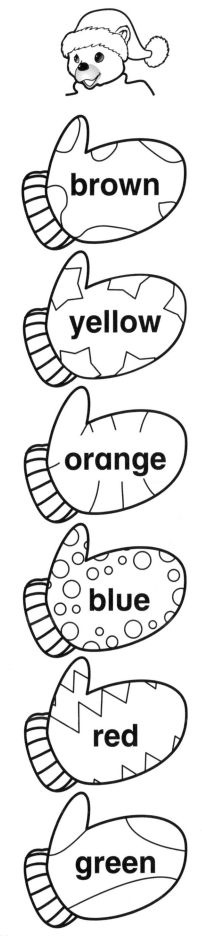

blue

brown

brown

yellow

red

orange

green

blue

yellow

red

orange

green

Name _____

Colorful Day

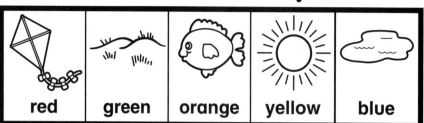

| red | green | orange | yellow | blue |

Color by the code.

Colorful Day

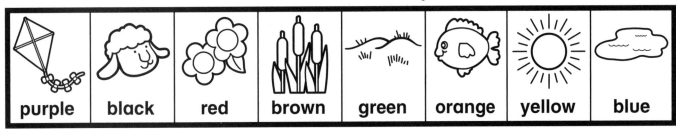

| purple | black | red | brown | green | orange | yellow | blue |

Color by the code.

Lucky Duck

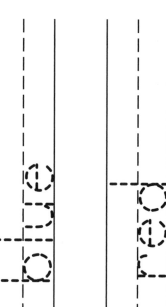

Color.

Trace the color word.

yellow

purple

blue

red

orange

green

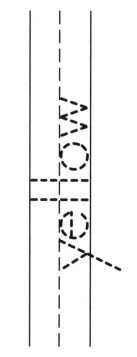

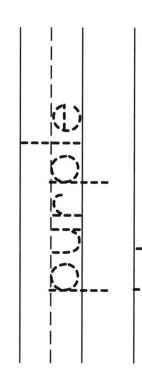

Name _____

Lucky Duck

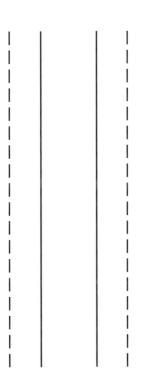

🖍 Color.

✏ Write the color word.

Color Words
red
yellow
green
orange
purple
blue

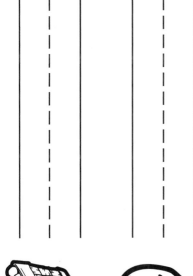

Feathery Favorites

 Color.

Trace.

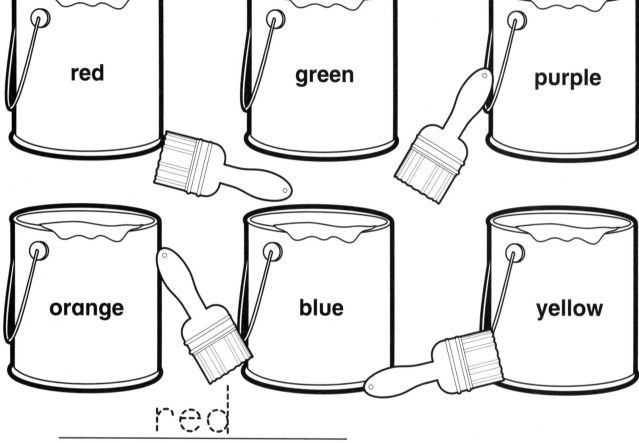

red

green

purple

orange

blue

yellow

red

green

purple

orange

blue

yellow

Feathery Favorites

🖍 Color.

✏ Write.

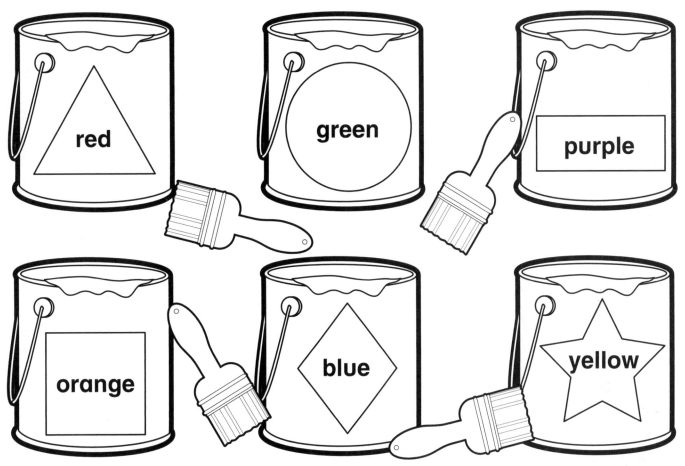

The △ is _____.

The ◯ is _____.

The ▭ is _____.

The ☆ is _____.

The ◇ is _____.

The ▢ is _____.

Counting Party Prizes

Read.   Trace the number. 🖍 Color.

three	
3	
one	
1	
five	
5	
two	
2	
four	
4	

Counting Party Prizes

Read. ✏️ Write the number. 🖍️ Color.

six	
three	
one	
five	
two	
four	

Windy Words

Read.   Count. ✏️ Color.

1	2	3	4	5
one	two	three	four	five

Color four.

Color three.

Color five.

Color two.

Color one.

Windy Words

Read. Count. Color.

Color six.

Color four.

Color three.

Color five.

Color two.

Color one.

Counting Sheep

Count the sheep .

Circle the correct number word.

six

two

nine

three

one

ten

six

eight

five

three

four

ten

Counting Sheep

Count the sheep .

Circle the correct number word.

six

two   five

nine

seven   three

one

five   ten

nine   six

eight

five

eight   three

four

six   ten

Super Snacks

🖍 Color. ✂ Cut. 🧴 Glue the pictures in order.

1	2	3	4

Name

Super Snacks

Color.

Cut.

Glue the pictures in order.

1	2	3	4

94

Busy Morning Bus Ride

Color.

Cut.

Glue the pictures in order.

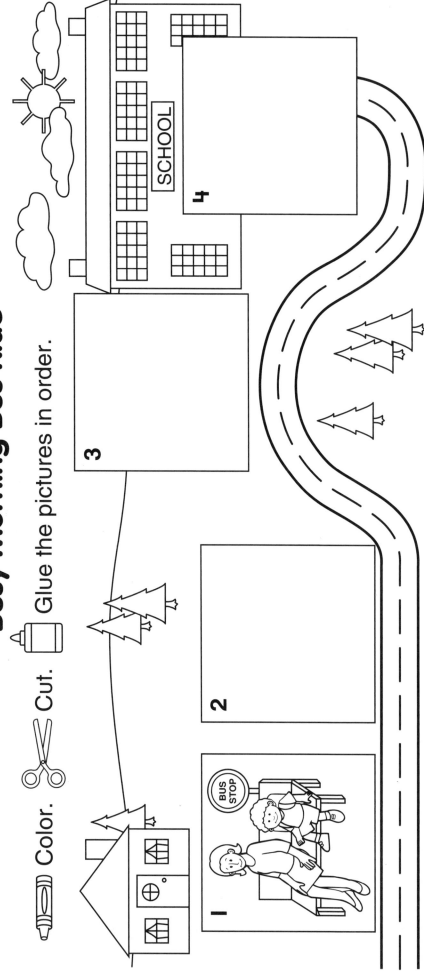

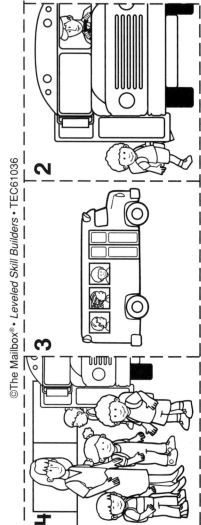

Name _____

Busy Morning Bus Ride

Color. Cut. Glue the pictures in order.

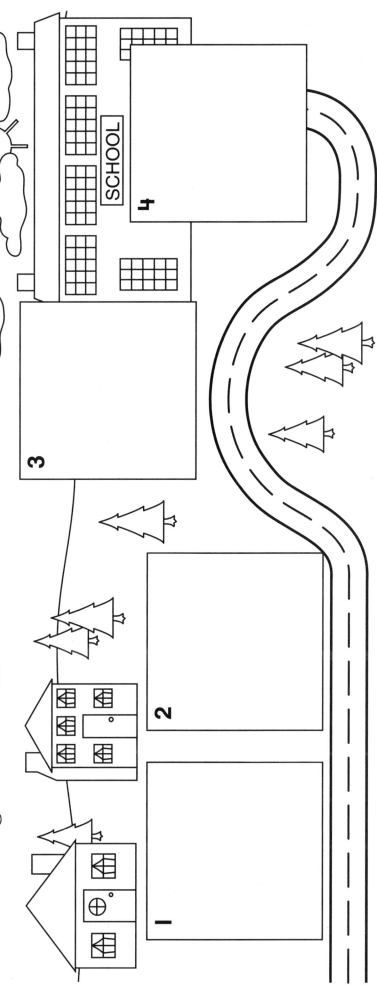

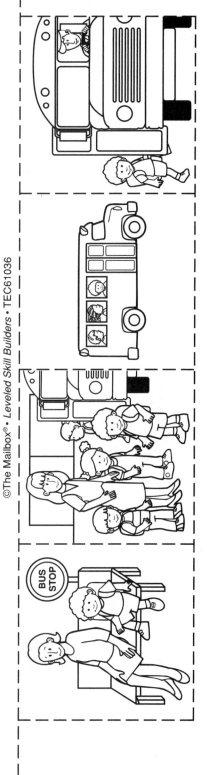

BUS STOP

Name _____

Fluttering Five

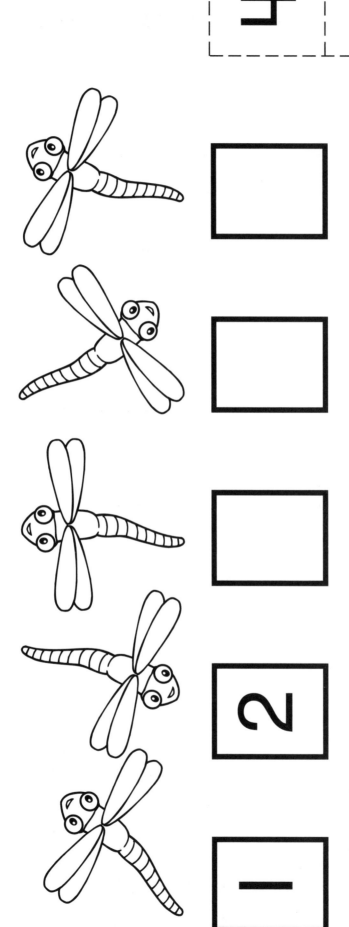

✂ Cut.

🖼 Glue the numbers in order.

| | | | 2 | 1 |

✏ Trace the numbers.

0 — 1 — 2 — 3 — 4 — 5

4

5

3

Name _____

Fluttering Five

 Cut. Glue the numbers in order.

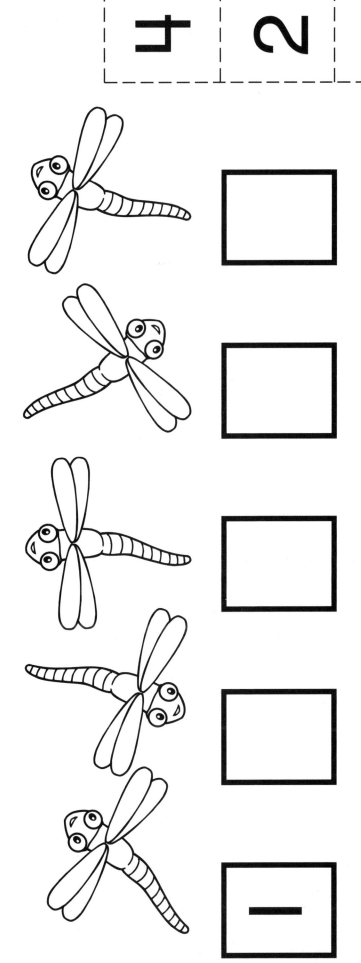

| 4 | 2 | 5 | 3 |

Write the numbers in order.

0 ————————— 5

97

Name _____

Ten for Lunch

✂ Cut. 🖊 Glue the numbers in order.

| 1 | 2 | | | 5 | | 7 | | | 10 |

✏ Trace the numbers.

0   1   2   3   4   5   6   7   8   9   10

9   4   8   3   6

Name _____

Ten for Lunch

✂️ Cut.   🫙 Glue the numbers in order.

						5		2	

✏️ Write the numbers in order.

0   1   ___   3   4   ___   ___   ___   ___   10

9	7	1	10	8	3
	4				6

Jumpin' Joeys

✂ Cut.

Glue the numbers in order.

| 1 | | 3 | 4 | | 6 | | 8 | | 10 |

©The Mailbox® • Leveled Skill Builders • TEC61036

9 5 5 2 7

Name _____

Jumpin' Joeys

Cut.

Glue the numbers in order.

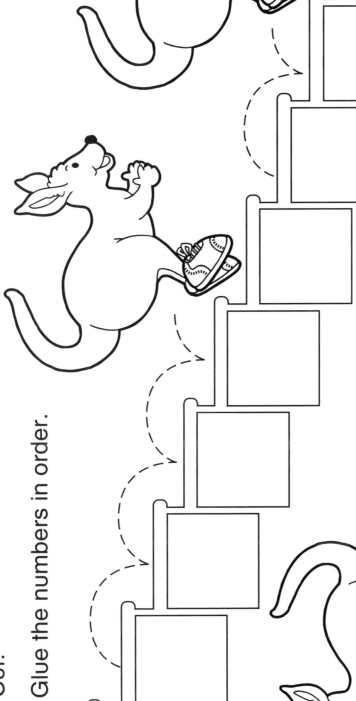

9 3 5 2 6 4 7 8

Name _____

Terrific Twenty

Trace the numbers in order.

2	3	4	5	6	7	8	9	10

Write the numbers in order.

Trace the numbers in order.

12	11	15	16	17	18	19	20

Write the numbers in order.

Name _____

Terrific Twenty

✏️ Write the numbers in order.

✏️ Draw a circle around each box with a 0.

🖍️ Color each box with a 5.

1		3			6		9	
12			15					20

What number comes next?

✏️ Write.

12, ___   6, ___   19, ___   3, ___

8, ___   10, ___   17, ___   14, ___

103

Name _____

Apple Goodies

 Count.

Cut. Glue.

6 six

2 two

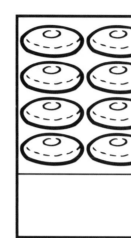

4 four

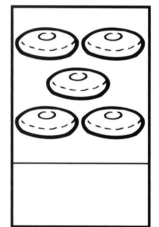

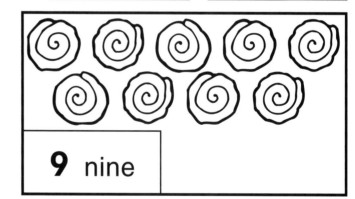

9 nine

1 one

3 three

5 five

7 seven

8 eight

10 ten

Name _____

Apple Goodies

Count.

Cut. Glue.

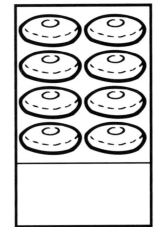

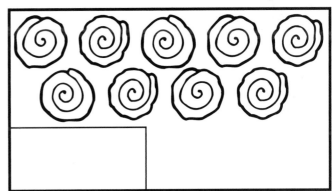

1 one	2 two	3 three	4 four	5 five	6 six	7 seven	8 eight	9 nine	10 ten

Chick's Picks

 Glue.

 Cut. Count to match.

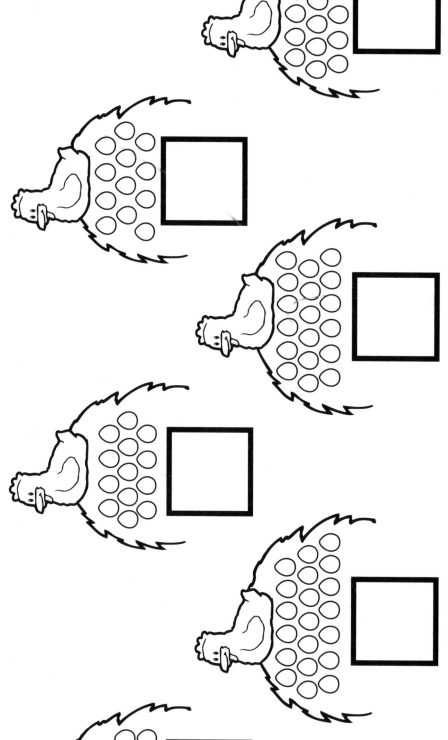

12	13	16	18	20

Name _____

Chick's Picks

✂ Cut. Count to match. 🧴 Glue.

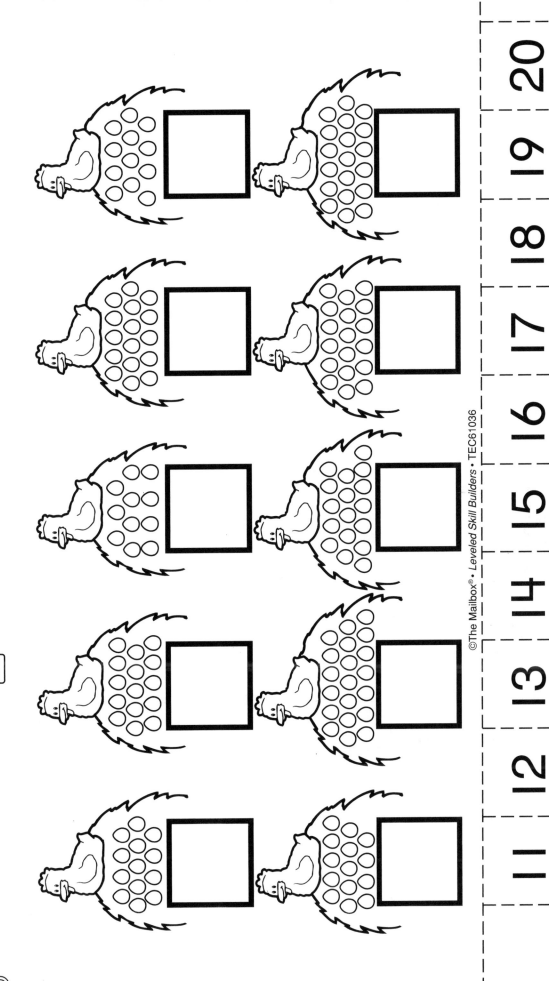

| 11 | 12 | 13 | 14 | 15 | 16 | 17 | 18 | 19 | 20 |

Have a Ball!

Color the **equal** sets.

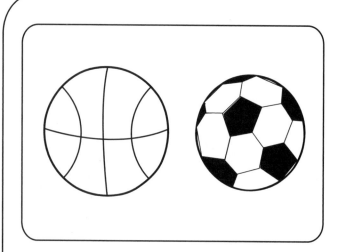

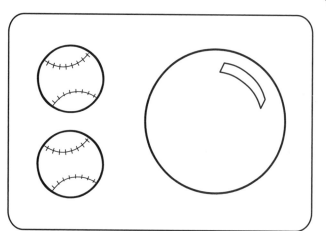

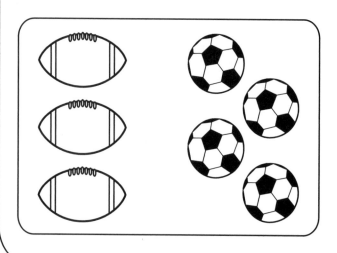

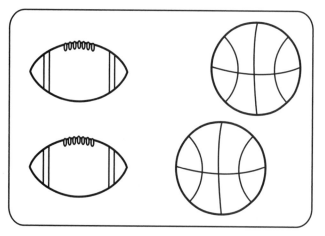

Name _____

Have a Ball!

Color the **equal** sets.

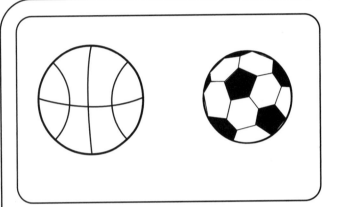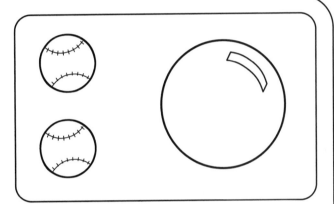

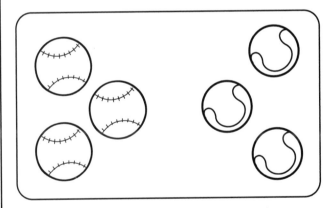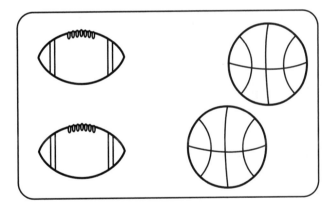

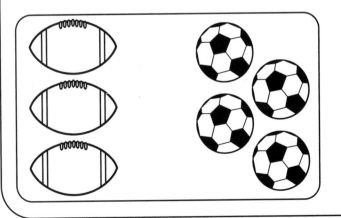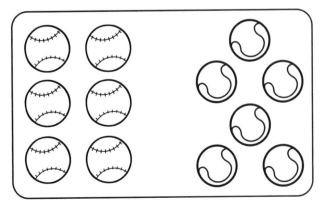

On the Move

Color the set that shows **more.**

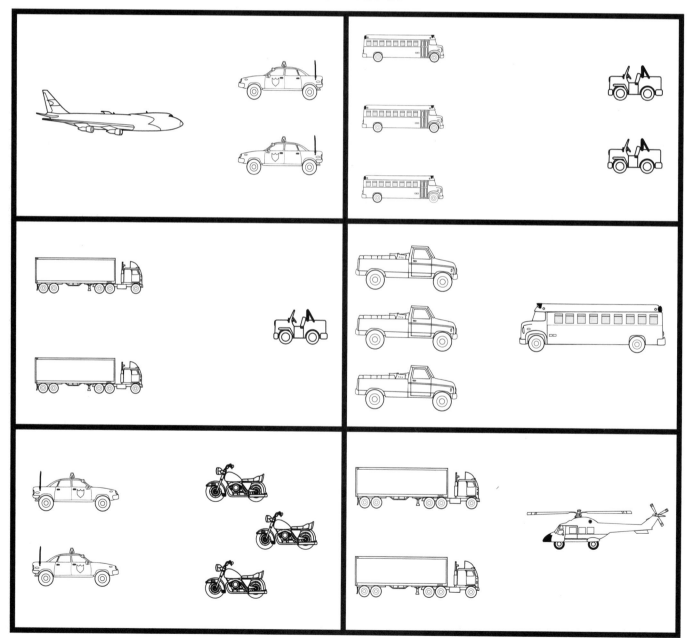

On the Move

Color the set that shows **more.**

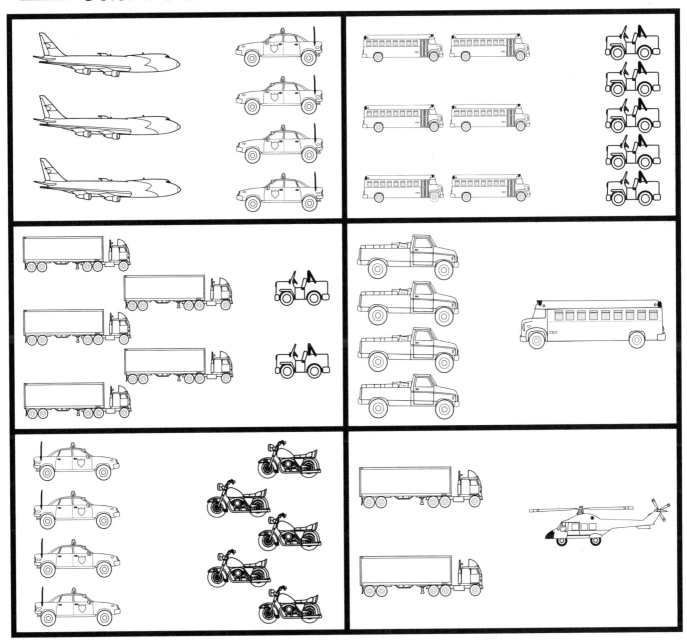

Ready, Set, Stamp

Color the set that shows **less.**

Ready, Set, Stamp

Color the set that shows **less**.

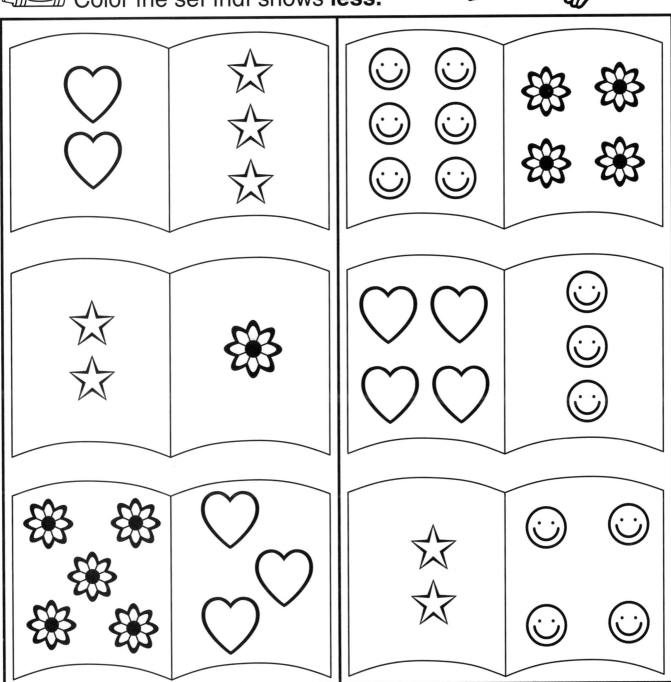

So Many Strawberries

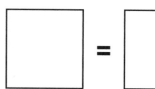

Write how many in the set.

Add.

$$\boxed{3} + \boxed{2} = \boxed{5}$$

$$\boxed{} + \boxed{} = \boxed{}$$

$$\boxed{} + \boxed{} = \boxed{}$$

$$\boxed{} + \boxed{} = \boxed{}$$

$$\boxed{} + \boxed{} = \boxed{}$$

 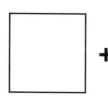

$$\boxed{} + \boxed{} = \boxed{}$$

So Many Strawberries

 Write how many in the set.

Add.

□ + □ = □   □ + □ = □

     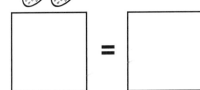

□ + □ = □   □ + □ = □

  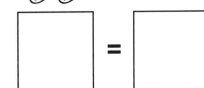  

□ + □ = □   □ + □ = □

  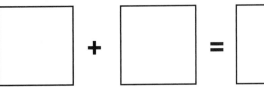

□ + □ = □   □ + □ = □

Hooray for the USA!

Add.

 Color by the code.

Color Code

3—red   4—white   5—blue

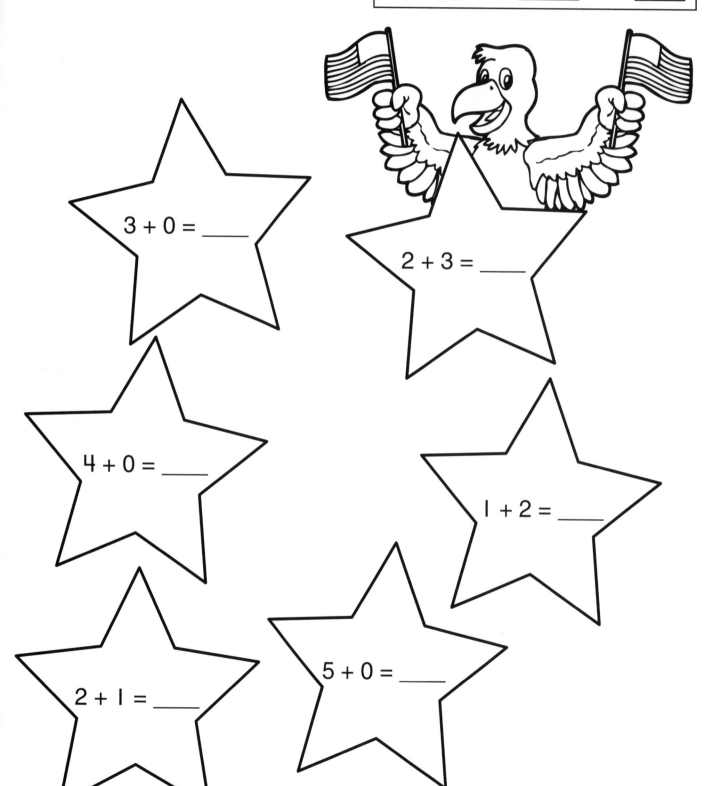

3 + 0 = ____

2 + 3 = ____

4 + 0 = ____

1 + 2 = ____

2 + 1 = ____

5 + 0 = ____

Name _____

Hooray for the USA!

Add.

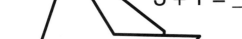 Color by the code.

$3 + 1 = $ ____

$3 + 0 = $ ____

$2 + 3 = $ ____

$4 + 0 = $ ____

$1 + 2 = $ ____

$5 + 0 = $ ____

$4 + 1 = $ ____

$2 + 2 = $ ____

$2 + 1 = $ ____

$3 + 2 = $ ____

Bunches of Blueberries

 Write how many in each set.

Add.

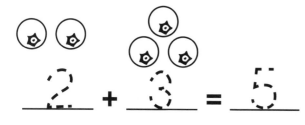 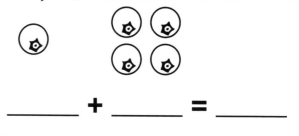

__2__ + __3__ = __5__   _____ + _____ = _____

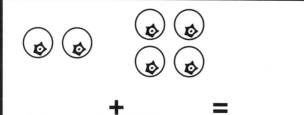 

_____ + _____ = _____   _____ + _____ = _____

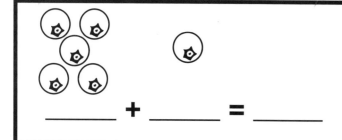 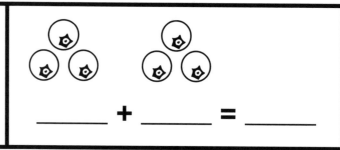

_____ + _____ = _____   _____ + _____ = _____

Bunches of Blueberries

 Write how many in each set.

Add.

_____ + _____ = _____

_____ + _____ = _____

_____ + _____ = _____

_____ + _____ = _____

_____ + _____ = _____

_____ + _____ = _____

_____ + _____ = _____

_____ + _____ = _____

_____ + _____ = _____

_____ + _____ = _____

Name _____

Pick of the Patch

Add.

✏️ Color by the code.

Color Code
7—yellow 5—red
6—blue 4—green
  3—brown

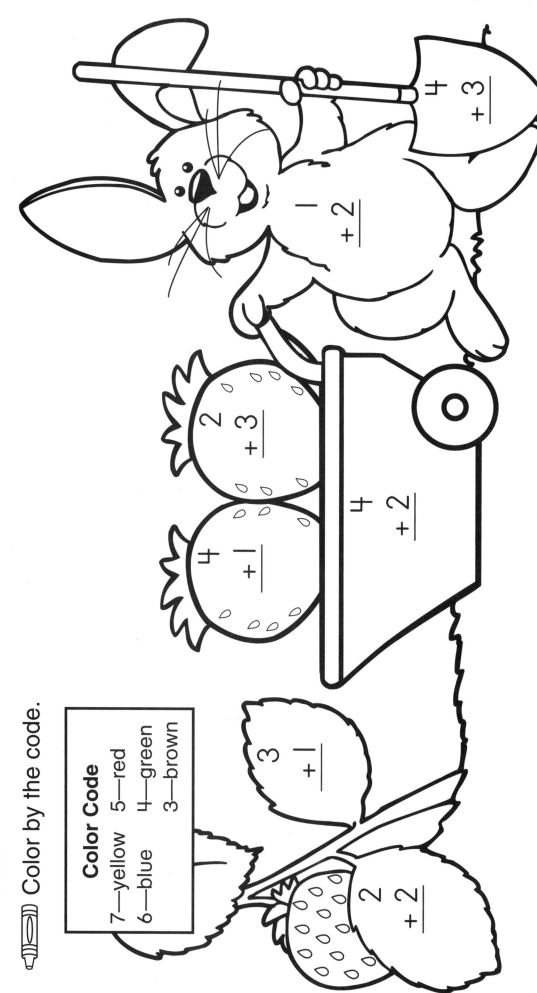

$$\begin{array}{r} 1 \\ +\ 2 \\ \hline \end{array}$$

$$\begin{array}{r} 4 \\ +\ 3 \\ \hline \end{array}$$

$$\begin{array}{r} 2 \\ +\ 3 \\ \hline \end{array}$$

$$\begin{array}{r} 4 \\ +\ 1 \\ \hline \end{array}$$

$$\begin{array}{r} 4 \\ +\ 2 \\ \hline \end{array}$$

$$\begin{array}{r} 3 \\ +\ 1 \\ \hline \end{array}$$

$$\begin{array}{r} 2 \\ +\ 2 \\ \hline \end{array}$$

Pick of the Patch

Add.

Color by the code.

Color Code
7—yellow 5—red 4—green
6—blue 3—brown

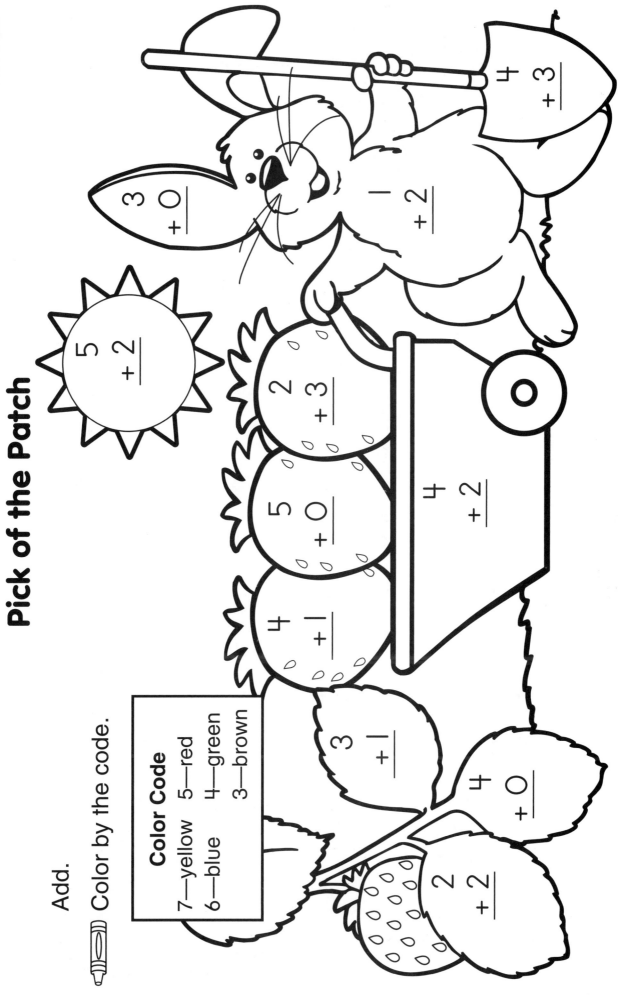

$$\begin{array}{r} 4 \\ +3 \\ \hline \end{array}$$

$$\begin{array}{r} 3 \\ +0 \\ \hline \end{array}$$

$$\begin{array}{r} 1 \\ +2 \\ \hline \end{array}$$

$$\begin{array}{r} 5 \\ +2 \\ \hline \end{array}$$

$$\begin{array}{r} 2 \\ +3 \\ \hline \end{array}$$

$$\begin{array}{r} 5 \\ +0 \\ \hline \end{array}$$

$$\begin{array}{r} 4 \\ +1 \\ \hline \end{array}$$

$$\begin{array}{r} 4 \\ +2 \\ \hline \end{array}$$

$$\begin{array}{r} 3 \\ +1 \\ \hline \end{array}$$

$$\begin{array}{r} 4 \\ +0 \\ \hline \end{array}$$

$$\begin{array}{r} 2 \\ +2 \\ \hline \end{array}$$

Simply Seeds

Add.

Color the matching seeds below.

$$\begin{array}{r} 2 \\ +\ 1 \\ \hline 3 \end{array}$$

$$\begin{array}{r} 6 \\ +\ 0 \\ \hline \end{array}$$

$$\begin{array}{r} 4 \\ +\ 4 \\ \hline \end{array}$$

$$\begin{array}{r} 3 \\ +\ 2 \\ \hline \end{array}$$

$$\begin{array}{r} 2 \\ +\ 2 \\ \hline \end{array}$$

$$\begin{array}{r} 6 \\ +\ 4 \\ \hline \end{array}$$

$$\begin{array}{r} 4 \\ +\ 5 \\ \hline \end{array}$$

$$\begin{array}{r} 1 \\ +\ 4 \\ \hline \end{array}$$

$$\begin{array}{r} 5 \\ +\ 2 \\ \hline \end{array}$$

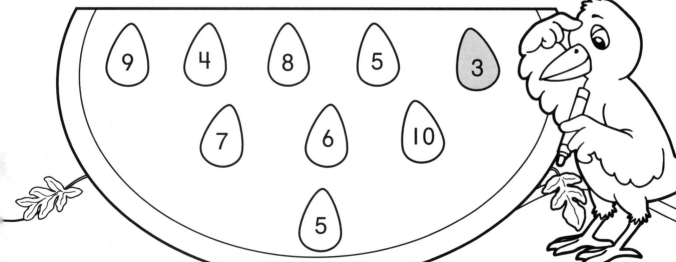

Simply Seeds

Add.

 Color the matching seeds below.

2	6	4	4
+ 1	+ 0	+ 4	+ 0

3	2	7	3
+ 2	+ 2	+ 0	+ 3

4	1	5	6
+ 5	+ 4	+ 2	+ 4

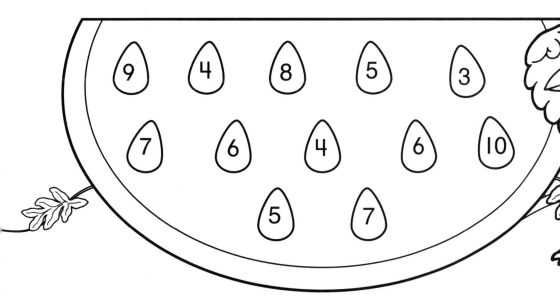

Take Flight

 Color the object that is shorter.

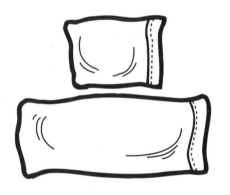

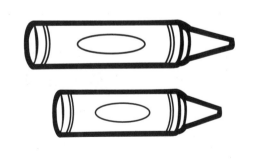

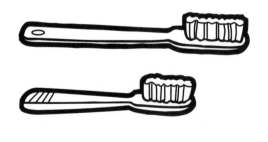

Take Flight

Color the object that is shorter.

All Aboard

Color the object that is longer.

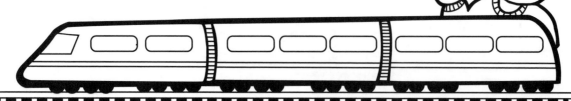

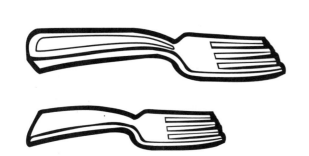

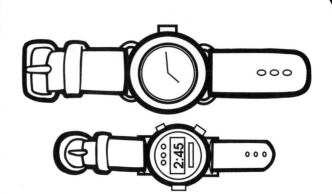

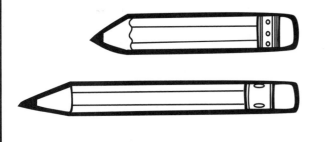

All Aboard

Color the object that is longer.

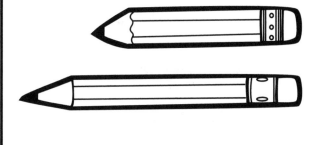

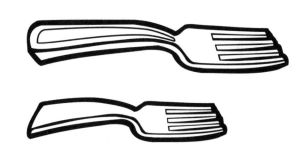

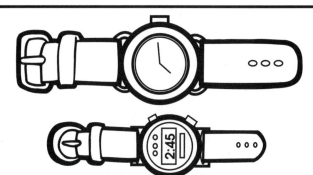

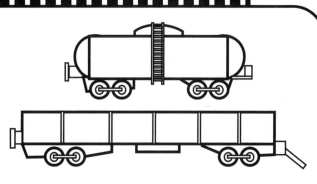

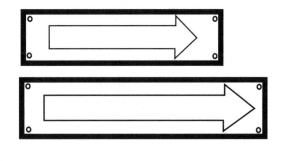

Penny for a Pickle

 Cut.

Glue a penny on each pickle.

©The Mailbox® • *Leveled Skill Builders* • TEC61036

Penny for a Pickle

    Cut.

Glue a penny on each pickle.

©The Mailbox® • *Leveled Skill Builders* • TEC61036

Ketchup or Mustard?

  Color the nickels red.

Color the other coins yellow.

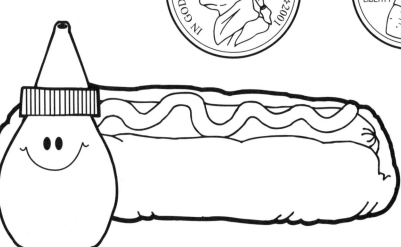

Ketchup or Mustard?

Color the nickels red.

Color the other coins yellow.

Double "Deli-icious"

Color by the code.

yellow

orange

green

Double "Deli-icious"

Color by the code.

yellow

orange

green

Name _____

Sunny Time

Color. Cut. Glue. Write.

It is ____ o'clock.

©The Mailbox® • *Leveled Skill Builders* • TEC61036

| 7 | 8 | 5 | 10 | 4 | 11 |

Sunny Time

 Color. ✂ Cut. 🔖 Glue. ✏ Write.

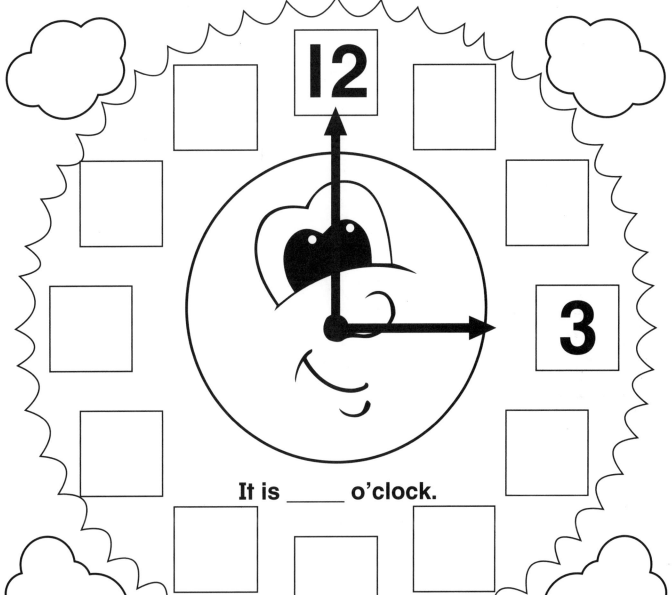

It is _____ o'clock.

7	2	5	1	4
9	6	8	10	11

Hour Power

 Cut.

Glue to show the correct time.

| 3:00 | |

©The Mailbox® • *Leveled Skill Builders* • TEC61036

| 8:00 | 5:00 | 7:00 |
| 2:00 | 1:00 | |

Hour Power

 Cut.

Glue to show the correct time.

©The Mailbox® • *Leveled Skill Builders* • TEC61036

8:00	5:00	9:00	7:00
2:00	11:00	3:00	1:00

Name _____

Colorful Shapes

 Color by the code.

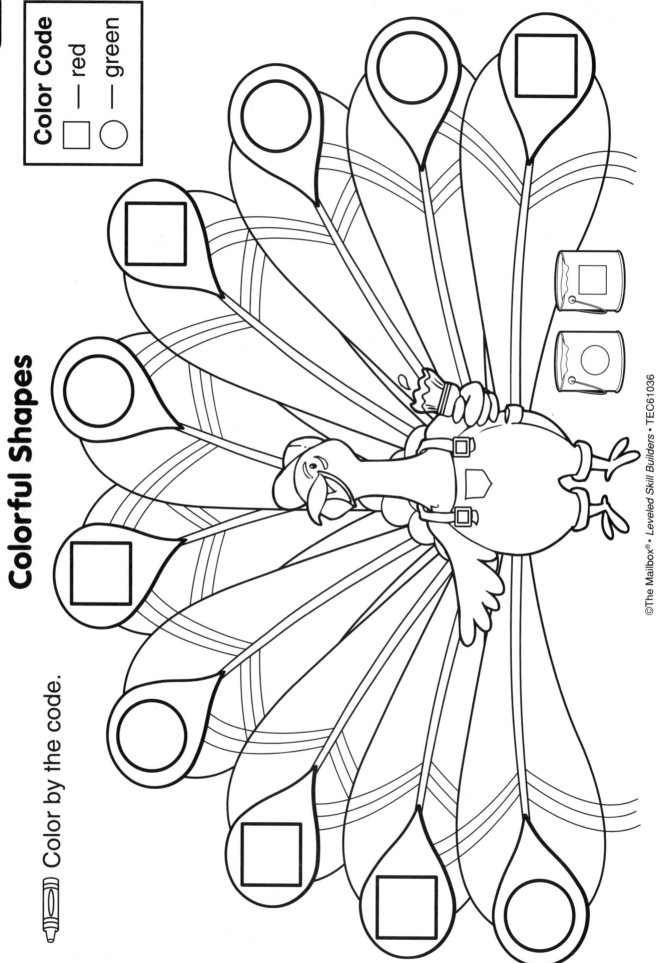

Name _____

Colorful Shapes

🖍 Color by the code.

Color Code
☐ — red
△ — blue
◯ — green

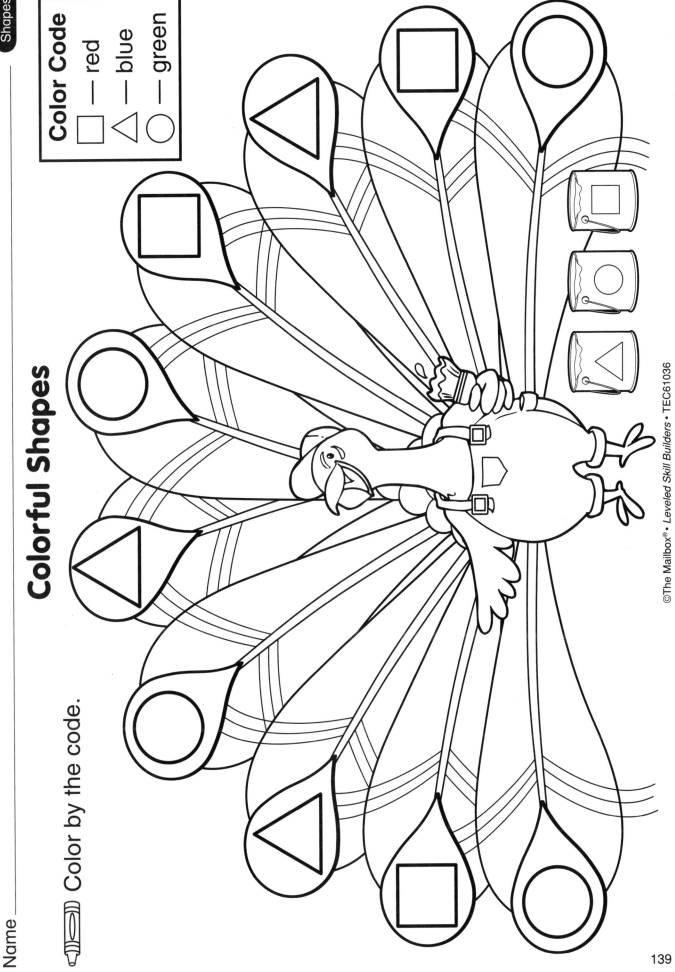

Name _____

Painting Peacock

©The Mailbox® • Leveled Skill Builders • TEC61036

Color Code

▭ — orange
☆ — purple

🖍 Color by the code.

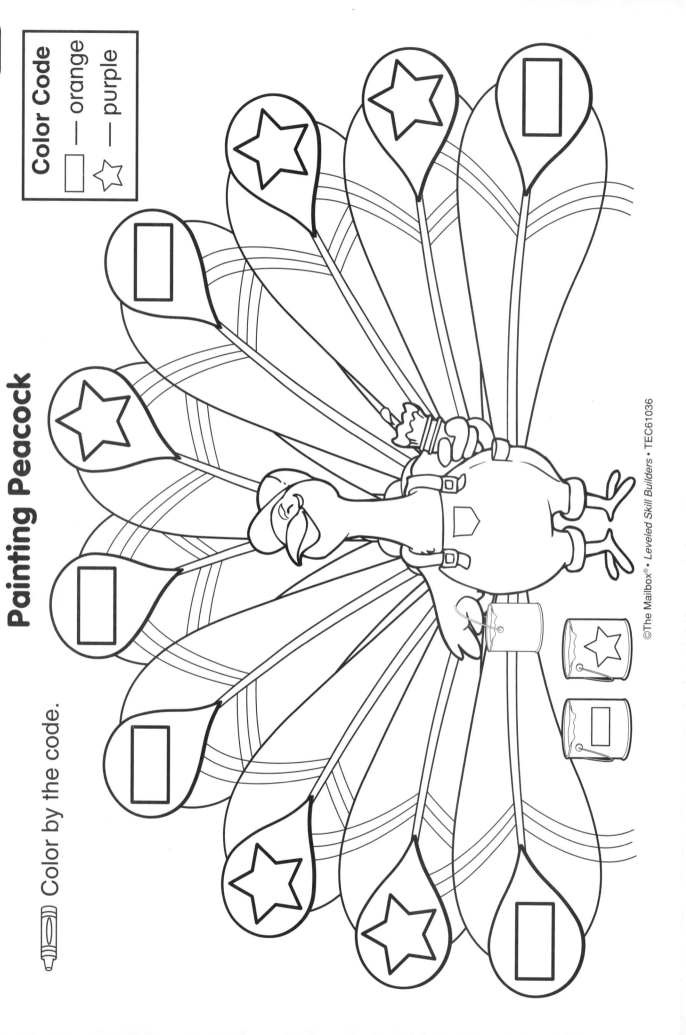

Name _____

Painting Peacock

🖍 Color by the code.

Color Code

▭ — orange
◇ — yellow
☆ — purple

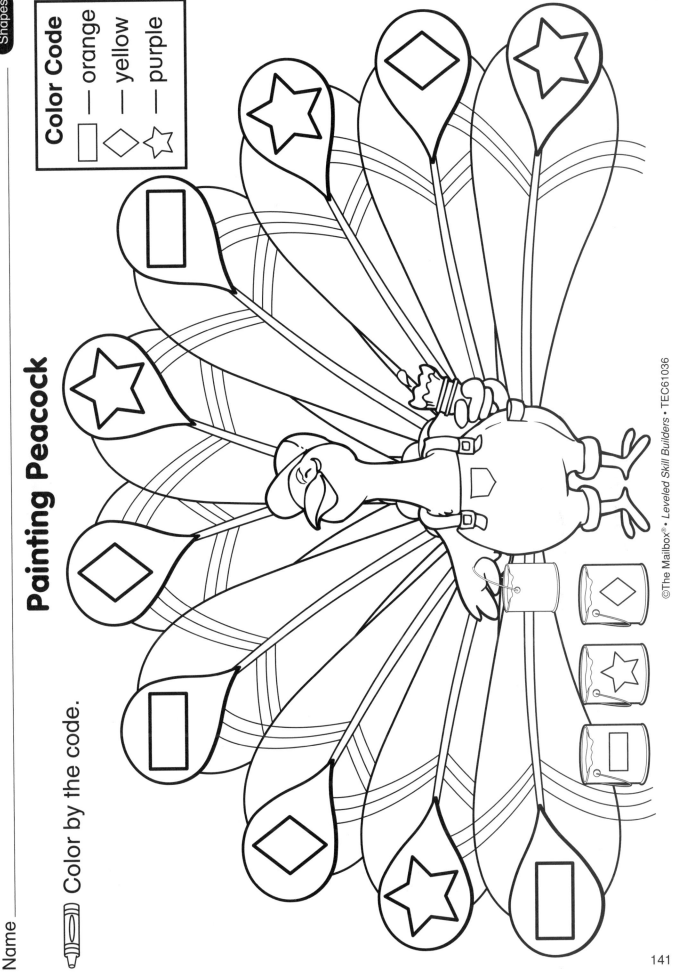

His and Hers

 Cut.

Graph.

 Glue.

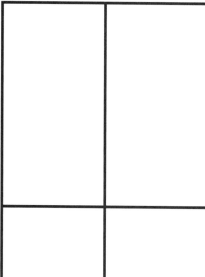

Write.

How many ? _____

How many ? _____

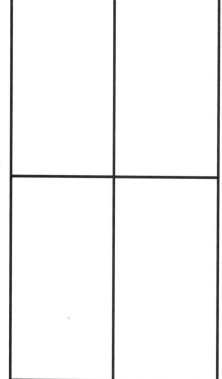

Name _____

His and Hers

 Cut.

Graph.

 Glue.

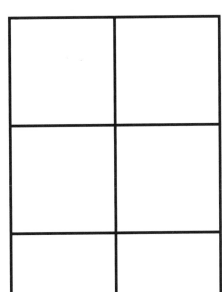

 Write.

How many 🐭 ? _____

How many 🐭 ? _____

©The Mailbox® • *Leveled Skill Builders* • TEC61036

143

Just Buggy

  Count.

🖍 Color the graph to show how many.

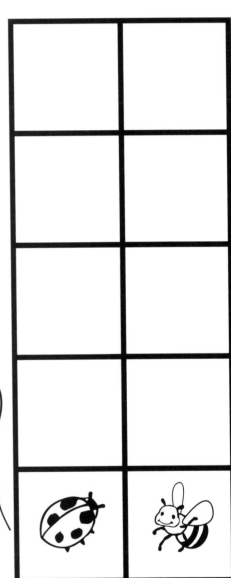

✏ Write.

How many ? _____

How many ? _____

Which has more? Color.

Name _____

Just Buggy

 Count.

 Color the graph to show how many.

Write.

How many ? _____

How many ? _____

Which has more? Color.

Down by the Pond

Count.

Color the graph to show how many.

Write.

How many more 🐸 than 🐢? _____

How many more 🐟 than 🐢? _____

How many 🐸, 🐢, and 🐟 in all? _____

Name _____

Down by the Pond

 Count.

Color the graph to show how many.

Write.

How many more than ? _____

How many more than ? _____

How many , , and  in all? _____

Vroom, Vroom!

 Cut.

Sort by size. Glue.

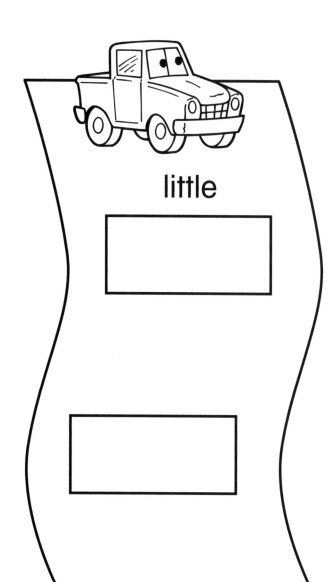

little

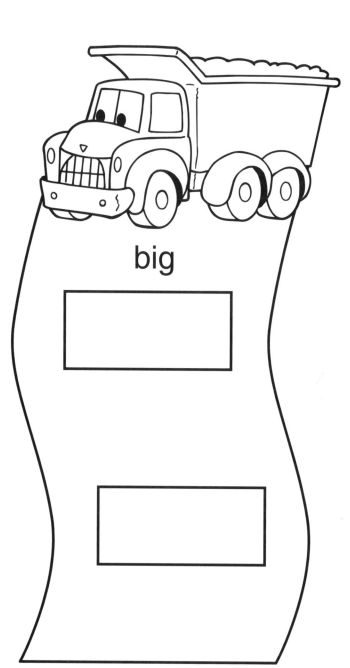

big

Name _____

Vroom, Vroom!

 Cut.

Sort by size. Glue.

little   big

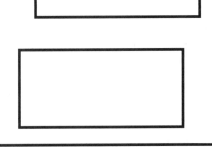

   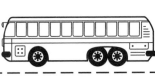

   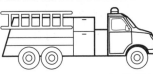

Baker's Bounty

Cut and sort.

Glue.

Name _____

Baker's Bounty

Cut and sort.

Glue.

Marble Matching

 Cut. Glue to match each set.

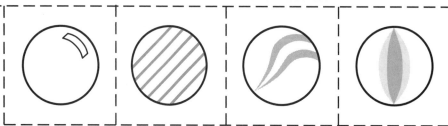

Marble Matching

 Cut. Glue to match each set.

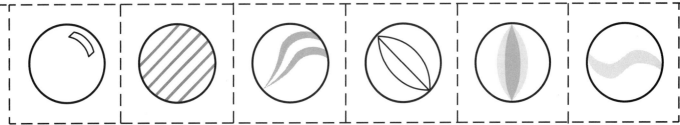

Name _____

Tasty Treats

 Cut.

Glue to finish the pattern.

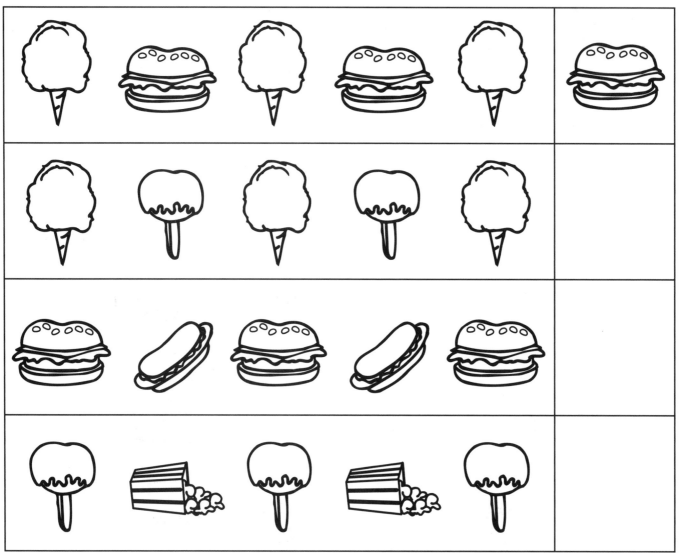

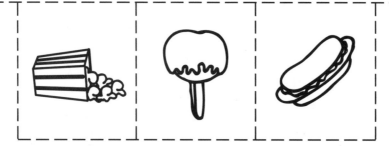

Tasty Treats

 Cut.

Glue to finish the pattern.

Name _____

Eraser Chasers

 Cut. Glue to finish the pattern.

 Color.

©The Mailbox® • *Leveled Skill Builders* • TEC61036

 156

Name_____

Eraser Chasers

 Cut.  Glue to finish the pattern.

Color.

Critter Counters

 Cut. Glue to finish the pattern.

 Color.

Name_____

Critter Counters

 Cut. Glue to finish the pattern.

Color.

159

Student Performance Cards and Award
Copy, cut out, and staple to students' completed work.

Look at Me
I'm hoppin' along
in my work!

TEC61036

"Ribbit-ing" Work!

Please review at home.

TEC61036

Award

CONGRATULATIONS!

_____
student

is making
great leaps
with

_____
skill

_____   _____
date   teacher

TEC61036